**Collins**

# Key Stage 3

# Geographical Enquiry

Student Book 2

**David Weatherly**
**Nicholas Sheehan**
**Rebecca Kitchen**

T0340451

William Collins' dream of knowledge for all began with the publication of his first book in 1819. A self-educated mill worker, he not only enriched millions of lives, but also founded a flourishing publishing house. Today, staying true to this spirit, Collins books are packed with inspiration, innovation and practical expertise. They place you at the centre of a world of possibility and give you exactly what you need to explore it.

Collins. Freedom to teach

Published by Collins
An imprint of HarperCollins*Publishers* Ltd
Westerhill Road
Bishopbriggs
Glasgow G64 2QT
www.harpercollins.co.uk

HarperCollins Publishers
Macken House
39/40 Mayor Street Upper
Dublin 1, D01 C9W8
Ireland

**Browse the complete Collins catalogue at www.collinseducation.com**

First edition 2015
© HarperCollins*Publishers* Limited 2015
Maps © Collins Bartholomew Ltd 2015

20 19 18 17 16

ISBN 978-0-00-741116-0

MIX
Paper
FSC
www.fsc.org  FSC™ C007454

A catalogue record for this book is available from the British Library

Typeset, designed, edited and proofread by Palimpsest Book Production Ltd, Falkirk, Stirlingshire
Cover designs by Angela English

Printed in Great Britain by Ashford Colour Ltd.

The mapping in this publication is generated from Collins Bartholomew digital databases.
Collins Bartholomew, the UK's leading independent geographical information supplier, can provide a digital, custom, and premium mapping service to a variety of markets.
For further information:
Tel: +44 (0)208 307 4515
e-mail: collinsbartholomew@harpercollins.co.uk

Visit our websites at: www.collins.co.uk or www.collinsbartholomew.com

If you would like to comment on any aspect of this book, please contact us at the above address or online.
e-mail: collinsmaps@harpercollins.co.uk

# Contents

# About this book

Meet Eratosthenes, the so-called 'father of geography'. Eratosthenes lived in Greece about 2200 years ago and is reputed to be the first person in the world to have used the word 'geography' and to call himself a 'geographer'. You could say that he invented geography – well, at least the study of the subject – which you are continuing happily with today. Amongst other things, Eratosthenes calculated the angle of tilt of the earth's axis and managed to measure the circumference of the world to an amazing degree of accuracy.

Eratosthenes asked and investigated the same questions that geographers pose today, such as:

• *Where are things located in the world?*

• *Why are they located where they are?*

• *How are people interacting with the environments in which they live?*

Incredibly, one of the first depictions of the 'known world' was drawn onto the side of a clay tablet by people living in the city of Babylon – in what is now the country of Iraq – about 300 years before Eratosthenes, the first geographer, was born. Modern geographers have analysed this ancient map and compared it with the current environment around Sippar, where it was found. The city of Babylon is at the centre of the engraving with seven other cities shown by small circles around it. The two larger outer circles almost certainly enclose an area of sea or ocean as they are labelled 'river of bitter water', whilst the two parallel lines at the bottom represent large marshland areas. The Zagros range of mountains is shown by two curved lines coming from the northeast and three named islands are shown as triangles just beyond the outer ring depicting the salt water. One of these islands is considered to be so far away and inaccessible that it has been evocatively named 'beyond the flight of birds'.

Today, specialist medical geographers are working alongside epidemiologists using computer modelling, Geographic Information Systems (GIS) and remote sensing to understand the factors determining the global distribution and spread of the Ebola virus. Geographers are needed because the origin and diffusion of infectious diseases are always associated with geographical factors such as place and location. Other factors that geographers consider when studying the geographical aspects of health and disease include environmental conditions, such as levels of heat and humidity, as well as the nature of population movements across an increasingly globalised world. Because geographers analyse people–environment relationships, their skills are proving invaluable in tracking the spread of Ebola and recommending ways in which the disease can be managed effectively around the world.

*'Infectious diseases can spread fast and far, and charting a carrier's movements is a key element of epidemiology. An old medical truism is that a patient's own story about their lifestyle is eighty percent of the diagnosis. Today that includes geography more than ever.'*

*Lydia Breunig, a geographer and Director of Special Projects, University of Arizona*

▶▶

**The spread of Ebola in the world in 2014**

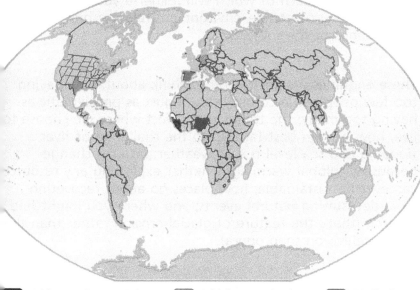

- ■ Widespread transmission
- ■ Local transmission – deaths
- ■ Local transmission – no deaths
- ◎ Initial cases – deaths
- ▢ Initial cases – no deaths
- ■ Medically evacuated cases – deaths
- ■ Medically evacuated cases – no deaths

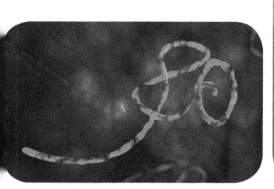

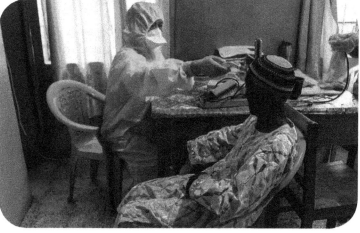

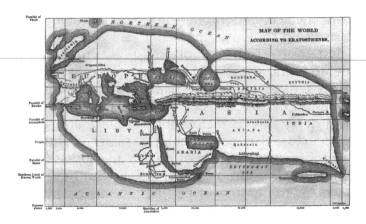

Although 2300 years separates Eratosthenes and modern day geographers like you, the questions we ask about the world and the manner in which we investigate them remain unchanged. In this book, we invite you to investigate another seven questions about the geography of the modern world, each of which will immerse you in the understanding of people–environment relationships – the very essence of the subject.

These enquiries will invite you to think about: why having too few people in a country can be just as problematic as having too many; the things that affect where we choose to live; how we can best face up to the challenge of river flooding and sea level rise as weather patterns change because of global warming; whether exploiting any resource can ever be sustainable; how places go about recovering from devastating natural events; and where you might find a *corrie* (that's the feature of glacial erosion rather than the British television soap opera).

As you ask questions and make sense of the world around you, we hope also that from time to time you might feel a connection between you and Eratosthenes, stretching back over two millennia.

Maybe you will end up like Eratosthenes, with a crater on the moon named after you for being a famous geographer – or, more likely, a currently undiscovered moon orbiting a yet-to-be-glimpsed planet. Eratosthenes would not recognise much of the world of today but he would be reassured that geographers are asking exactly the same questions of it as he did. People and the environments in which they live and upon which they depend may change over time, but the spirit and purpose of geography always remains the same.

David Weatherly | Nicholas Sheehan | Rebecca Kitchen

# Where in the world will your enquiries take you?

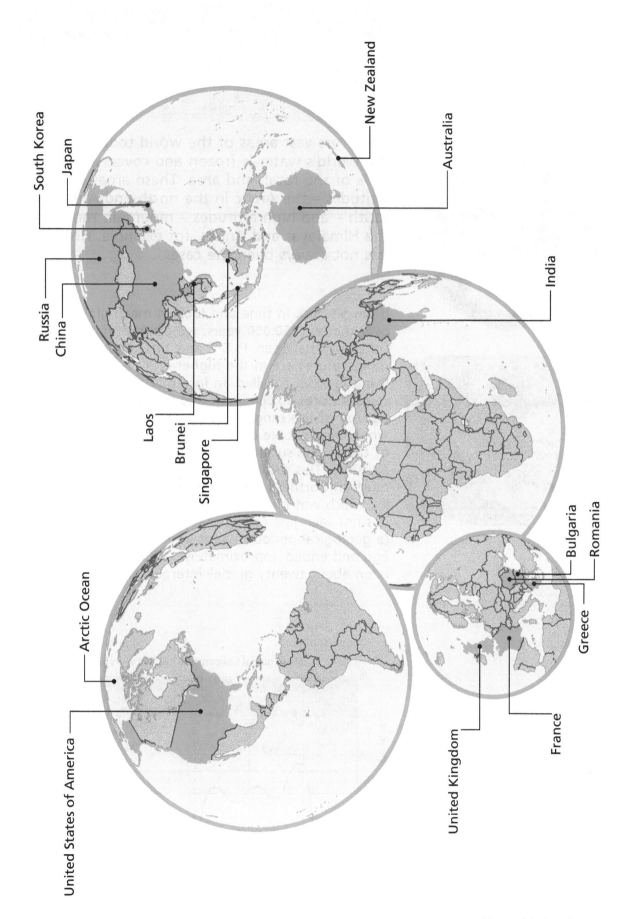

South Korea
Japan
New Zealand
Australia
Russia
China
India
Laos
Brunei
Singapore
Arctic Ocean
Bulgaria
Romania
Greece
United States of America
France
United Kingdom

# 1 Frozen landscapes

## Do corries really prefer north facing slopes?

Ice covers vast areas of the world today; about 5% of the world's water is frozen and covers approximately 10% of the total land area. These areas exist at high latitudes – the Arctic in the north and Antarctica in the south – and high altitudes – mountain ranges such as the Himalayas and Andes, for example. However, this has not always been the case.

If we go back in time and look at mean global temperature over the last 150,000 years, we can see that it has fluctuated between 15.5°C and 11°C. Today, our temperatures are at the higher end of this range; we are living in what is called an **interglacial** period. If we look at temperatures 20,000 years ago we can see they are at the bottom of this range. This is known as a **glacial** period (or what some people call an Ice Age), where ice covers more of the earth's surface and extends to lower latitudes and altitudes. This means that during the last glacial period, much of northern Europe, including the UK, was covered in ice which was hundreds of metres thick. However, the earth has not seen just one glacial period. During the **Pleistocene** (a geological period of time which started 2.6 million years ago and ended approximately 11,700 years ago) there have been about twenty glacial–interglacial cycles.

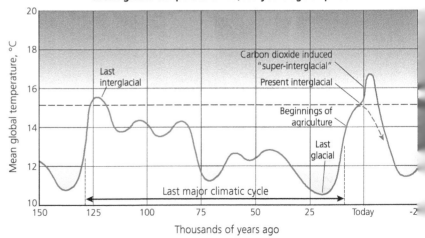

**Mean global temperature 150,000 years ago to present**

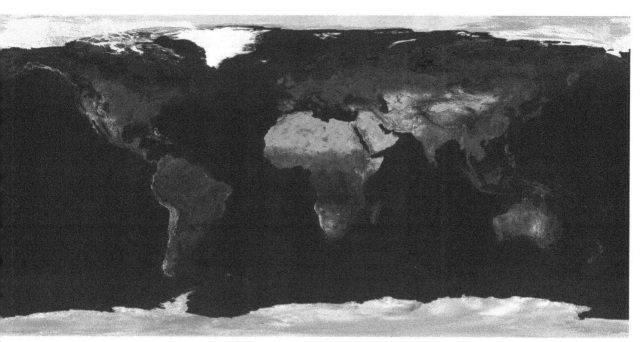

A map of ice coverage in the world in summer

A map of maximum extent ice coverage in Europe

Ice behaves in a way which makes it a very powerful agent of erosion which has helped to shape the landscape of Britain over tens of thousands of years. The ice in a glacier is so thick and heavy that a huge amount of pressure is exerted at the base and this melts the bottom couple of centimetres.

You can see this process in the picture of the glacier cross section (Figure A) – the bottom layer (which is about 20 cm) is more transparent than the layer above because it is in the process of melting. This meltwater reduces friction between the ice and the rock below so that the ice flows downhill like a frozen river.

Figure A: *Cross section of a glacier*

Contrary to what you might think, glaciers are not made of pure, frozen water like giant ice cubes. They have a huge amount of debris embedded within them of varying sizes. The sheer scale of the glacier means that it can carry a mixture of tiny particles and huge rocks the size of your classroom! So, instead, it is better to think of a glacier as a giant ice cube with sand and stones frozen into it. As the glacier flows over the landscape it erodes by two different methods: **abrasion** and **plucking**.

During glacial periods **freeze-thaw** weathering of the landscape occurs. Watch the animation at:

http://www.geolsoc.org.uk/ks3/gsl/education/resources/rockcycle/page4268.html

- Why do you think freeze-thaw weathering happens in glaciated areas?

- Can you describe what the fragments of rock which break off are like?

- How does this help us explain why the processes of erosion, such as abrasion, are so effective at changing the landscape?

Abrasion occurs when the sand and stones embedded in the glacier act like a piece of sandpaper, scratching and scouring the rock at its base. It leaves behind deep grooves called striations, which you can see in the picture of rocks in Mount Rainier National Park, USA (Figure A). These lines are also visible in the rocks in New York's Central Park as both of these areas were covered by ice during the last glacial period.

The other way in which ice erodes the landscape is through the process of plucking. Plucking happens when the rocks at the side or bottom of the glacier become frozen to the ice. The rock is attached to the ground, so cannot move, but the glacier continues to flow. This usually rips the rock away, leaving a jagged landscape. The best way to think of this is to consider what happens if you put an ice cube on your tongue and then suddenly pull it away (although it is best not to actually try this out as it hurts!).

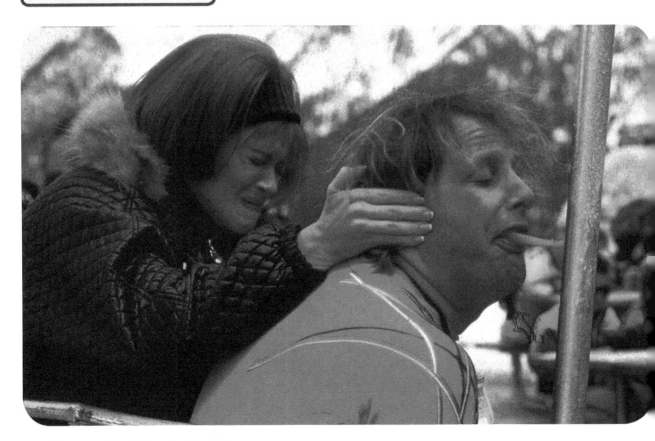

Figure A: *Striations*

## ► Consolidating your thinking ◄

Look at the diagram showing the ice flowing over the bedrock. Draw a sketch of this diagram. Can you add annotations to show which process of erosion is happening where, and how it operates? Can you add arrows to show the direction you think the ice is flowing in? Why do you think that it is flowing in this direction?

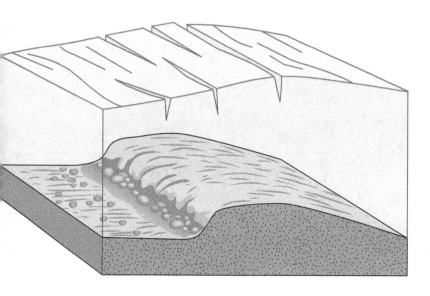

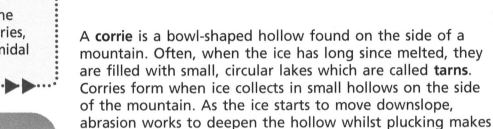

## 1.2 Which glacial landforms exist in upland areas and how are they formed?

Watch the short video at:

http://www.youtube.com/watch?v=EF4AHb4Lt_A

which explains the formation of corries, arêtes and pyramidal peaks in detail.

▶ ▶

In upland areas, the ice moves more easily due to gravity, so glaciers erode the landscape more effectively, creating dramatic scenery within which glaciers were created. There are three main landforms of erosion to be found in upland areas: corries, **arêtes** and **pyramidal peaks**.

A **corrie** is a bowl-shaped hollow found on the side of a mountain. Often, when the ice has long since melted, they are filled with small, circular lakes which are called **tarns**. Corries form when ice collects in small hollows on the side of the mountain. As the ice starts to move downslope, abrasion works to deepen the hollow whilst plucking makes the **backwall** steeper. You can see this in the diagram (Figure A).

When two corries form back-to-back they produce a steep, knife-edged ridge called an arête and when three or more corries form on the top of a mountain they create a classic pyramidal peak.

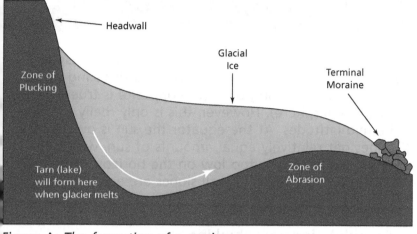

Figure A: *The formation of a corrie*

Labels in Figure A:
- Headwall
- Zone of Plucking
- Glacial Ice
- Terminal Moraine
- Tarn (lake) will form here when glacier melts
- Zone of Abrasion

Map label: Lake District

## ▶ Consolidating your thinking ◀

Can you make a storyboard to show the formation of a corrie out of modelling clay or building blocks?

Some of the most dramatic examples of corries in the UK are found in the Lake District and Snowdonia (although they are called 'cwms' in Wales). Carry out some research into one of these case studies and create a quiz about it. Some examples include Red Tarn and Easedale Tarn (Lake District) and Cwm Idwal (Snowdonia).

> The difference in temperature between north and south facing slopes is only a few degrees, but this is enough to make north facing slopes in the northern hemisphere a more likely location for corries to form. ►►

Due to the angle of the sun, in the northern **hemisphere** the influence of aspect tends to make north facing slopes cooler than south facing ones (the opposite is true in the southern hemisphere). However, this is only really the case in the mid-latitudes. At the equator the sun is overhead so all slopes get relatively equal amounts of sun, whilst at the poles the sun is usually too low on the horizon or moves around in a circle, so, again, all slopes are equally affected.

### ▷ Consolidating your thinking ◁

### Assessment: Chi-squared

You are going to carry out a statistical test – Chi-squared – to bring all of this information together and help you answer the key question at the beginning of the enquiry. You will work step-by-step through the activity in the Teacher Book (pp.8–11), use the information in this enquiry, plus additional reading of your own (additional sources are recommended in the side box below) to *demonstrate that you can understand* the geographical skills and processes which explain whether or not corries really prefer north facing slopes.

- The first thing that you need to do is to identify some corries on an Ordnance Survey map of Snowdonia (a colour version of the map is on the page opposite). If you want to challenge yourself, you may also want to try to spot examples of arêtes and a pyramidal peak (although the pyramidal peak in this example is much flatter than other examples and therefore doesn't really look like a pyramid!)

- You are then going to use the data for the fifty-six corries in Snowdonia to complete a rose diagram. Why do you think that this technique is the most appropriate for displaying the data? Can you think of any other data presentation techniques that might work as well?

- The next stage is to work through the Chi-squared calculation on the worksheet, which will help you to determine whether the orientation of corries in Snowdonia is random or not. You will need a calculator to help you. Don't be put off by the difficult-looking equation. If you work through the steps slowly and make sure you understand what you have to do for each part of the table by looking at the examples that have been done for you, you should be fine. If you want to understand Chi-squared in a little more detail you can

**Additional sources of information to extend the depth and breadth of your explanation:**

http://www.grough.co.uk/magazine/2014/04/15/easter-hillwalkers-warned-its-still-winter-on-the-mountains

http://www.coolgeography.co.uk/A-level/AQA/Year%2012/Cold%20environs/Glacial%20Landforms/Landforms.htm

http://www.geography-site.co.uk/pages/physical/glaciers/origin.html

◄◄

look at http://www.cliffsnotes.com/math/statistics/bivariate-relationships/chi-square-x2 and check your understanding in the following quiz: http://www.cliffsnotes.com/math/statistics/bivariate-relationships/quiz-chi-square-x2.

- Finally, you will need to write a short paragraph which summarises whether or not corries prefer north facing slopes and why this might be. Make sure that you use a range of **geographical terminology** in your explanation, such as: corrie, plucking, abrasion, aspect, etc.

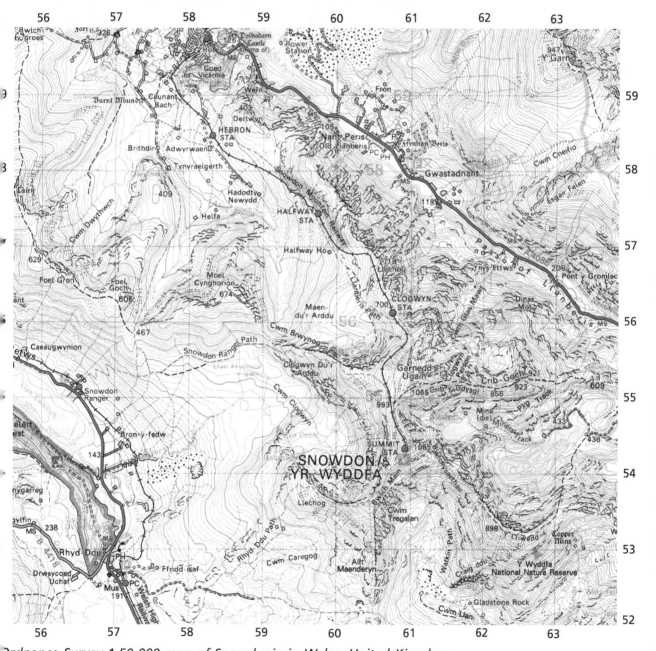

*Ordnance Survey 1:50 000 map of Snowdonia in Wales, United Kingdom*

### Extension

There are thirty-seven corries in the Lake District and their distribution can be seen in the table below.

**Number of corries in the Lake District by area**

| N | NE | E | SE | S | SW | W | NW |
|---|----|---|----|---|----|---|----|
| 8 | 13 | 7 | 5 | 4 | 0 | 0 | 0 |

Just by looking at the data, does the pattern appear similar or different to that which you observed for Snowdonia? Carry out the Chi-squared technique on the data for the Lake District using the steps in the Teacher Book (pp.8–11). Do you come to the same conclusion about whether corries prefer north facing slopes or not?

**Extending your enquiry** ▶▶

## 1.4 What other glacial landforms are there?

Corries, arêtes and pyramidal peaks are not the only landforms of erosion that are formed by glaciers. In lowland areas, glaciers bulldozed through the landscape, which was previously shaped by rivers, to create deep, U-shaped **glacial troughs**, **ribbon lakes** and **hanging valleys**. However, landforms of deposition – where the glacier starts to melt and drops the debris it has been carrying – are also common in lowland glaciated areas. The largest eroded material, mentioned in Question 1.1 on page 10, can sometimes be transported such massive distances that it comes to rest on bedrock that is a completely different geology. These huge boulders are called **erratics**, as they appear erratically scattered over the landscape. Smaller material is deposited at the bottom of glacial troughs and is shaped into **moraines** or **drumlins**.

## ▶ Consolidating your thinking ◀

Select one of the glacial landforms found in lowland areas below. Use the photograph of the landform to draw a fieldsketch. Look at http://www.rgs.org/OurWork/Schools/ Fieldwork+and+local+learning/Fieldwork+techniques/ Sketching+and+photography.htm and http://www.bbc.co.uk/ scotland/education/int/geog/limestone/field/index.shtml to help you. You may need to carry out some research so that your annotations are clear and detailed. Make sure that your annotations describe what the landform looks like as well as how it is formed.

Have a look at the fieldsketch of a drumlin in the Teacher Book (p.13). Do you think that the annotations are effective? Do they describe the shape of the drumlin and explain its formation clearly? What could be done to improve the fieldsketch?

Wainwright's Fells have been mapped by cartographer and geographer Peter Burgess using a similar technique to that which has been used to map the London Underground. The 'Tubular Fells' map opposite is a cartogram – a special type of map where a theme is used rather than land area or distance.

The Lake District, located in Northwest England, is a landscape which has been shaped by glaciers and contains many of the landforms explored in this enquiry. The area is popular with fell walkers and many of the peaks can be climbed by those with limited walking experience. Between 1955 and 1966, a man called Alfred Wainwright climbed the 214 Lake District peaks (ranging in height from 298–978 m) and described his adventures in a series of seven illustrated books. As a consequence, bagging 'the Wainwrights' has become a challenge for those with a love of fell walking.

According to the Long Distance Walkers Association, there are approximately 500 people who have climbed all 214 Wainwrights (including forty who have completed the challenge more than once!). The youngest person to have met the challenge was a boy of six years, four months and twenty-seven days, who climbed the last peak on his list in 2008.

Obviously, the Lake District is also famous for its lakes, and the ribbon lakes which were scoured out by glacial erosion lie at the bottom of the valleys. Perhaps the most famous is Lake Windermere, which, at 18 km in length, is the largest natural lake in England, although Ullswater, Buttermere and Wastwater are equally dramatic. Water sports, including canoeing, kayaking and sailing, are common and take advantage of the large expanse of water and spectacular views.

### ▶ Consolidating your thinking ◀

Imagine that you are going to spend a week on holiday in the Lake District. You want to do some fell walking and water sports but also want to see what the local towns have to offer. Use the sheets in the Teacher Book (pp.14–15) and the suggested websites to create a detailed itinerary for your holiday. You will also need to consider where you will stay, what you'll need to pack and what you'll do when it rains!

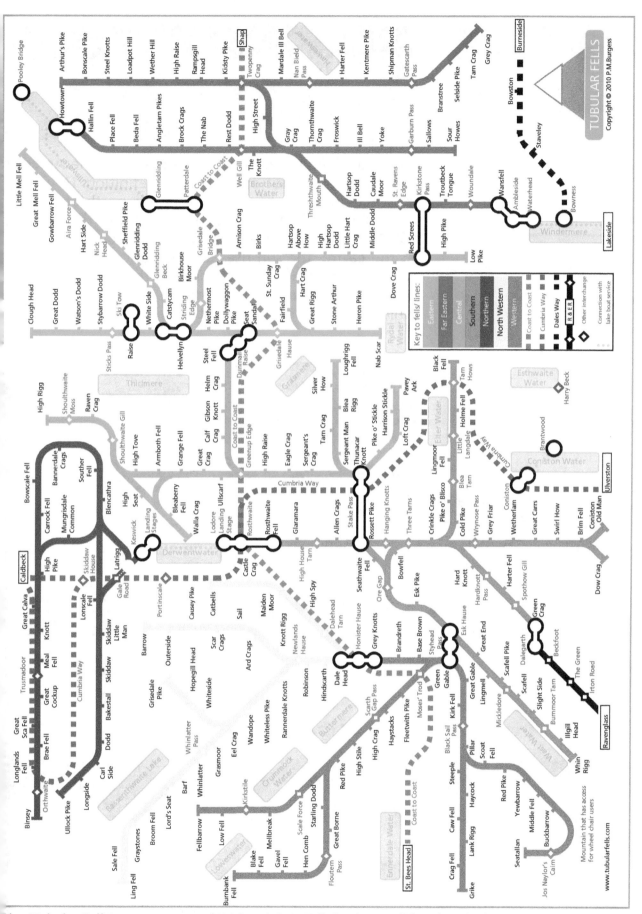

The 'Tubular Fells': a cartogram of Wainwright's Fells in the English Lake District

# 2 On thin ice

## Can Russia exploit the Arctic sustainably?

Trying to define exactly what we mean by 'the **Arctic**' is tricky as there is not one universal definition. However, most scientists identify it as the region north of the Arctic Circle, a line of latitude which circles the earth at 66° 33' N. At the North Pole (the most northern point of the earth), the sun rises and sets once per year, which means that there are six months of continuous daylight followed by six months of twilight during which total darkness may last for about eleven weeks!

The situation for the rest of the Arctic is not quite so extreme, but still there is at least one day per year which has no sun (polar night) and one day which has no night (midnight sun). Temperatures in the Arctic are cold in winter at about –40°C on average, although the coldest recorded temperature was –68°C, and cool in summer at below 10°C.

Rather than being a continental landmass like Antarctica, the Arctic is actually a vast ocean which is covered with floating sea ice. The ice moves around as it is blown by the wind and melts if temperatures rise much above freezing.

These conditions make it challenging to live in the Arctic, however approximately four million **indigenous people**, including the Inuit, have adapted to these conditions by developing warm homes and clothes and learning to navigate the sea ice.

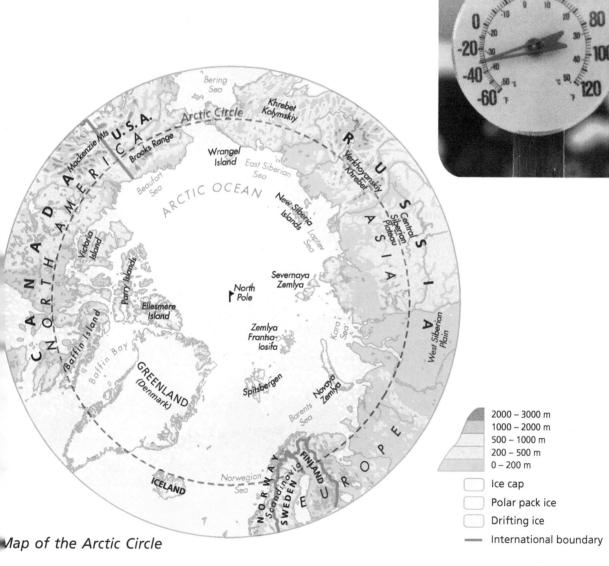

*Map of the Arctic Circle*

| | |
|---|---|
| | 2000 – 3000 m |
| | 1000 – 2000 m |
| | 500 – 1000 m |
| | 200 – 500 m |
| | 0 – 200 m |
| | Ice cap |
| | Polar pack ice |
| | Drifting ice |
| — | International boundary |

No country owns the North Pole or the area of the Arctic Ocean that surrounds it. However, the countries that border the Arctic Ocean – Canada, Denmark (via its territory in Greenland), Iceland, Norway, the USA and Russia – are allowed to claim territory up to 370 km (equal to 200 nautical miles) from their coasts as an **Exclusive Economic Zone (EEZ)**. Russia claims the largest area of the Arctic because approximately one-fifth of Russia lies north of the Arctic Circle and half of the four million people that live in the Arctic live in Russia.

Whilst this division seems relatively straightforward, it is made more complicated by the **United Nations Convention on the Law of the Sea (UNCLOS)**. Once a country signs the **treaty**, it has ten years to make claims to an extended continental shelf which, if proved, gives the country exclusive rights to any resources on or below the seabed. Russia signed the treaty in 1997, so had until 2007 to prove that the continent of Eurasia extended further into the Arctic Ocean.

**A diagram of extended continental shelf**

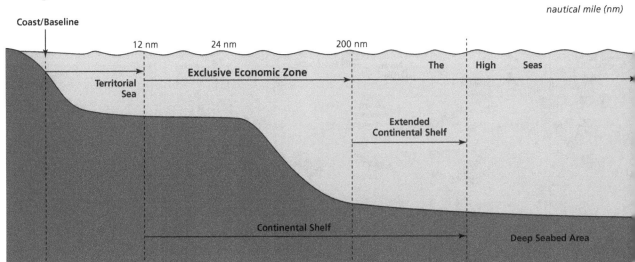

*The Russian polar expedition returns to Moscow after planting the Russian flag under the North Pole*

Read the article at:

http://news.bbc.co.uk/1/hi/world/europe/6927395.stm

which describes what happened in 2007 when a Russian expedition planted their national flag under the sea below the North Pole.

Add the North Pole and the Lomonosov Ridge to your map. Why do you think that countries are so keen to claim more territory in the Arctic?

Have a look at the cartoon at:

http://theglobaljournal.net/article/view/439/

to help you with your thinking.

In 2001, Russia claimed that the Lomonosov Ridge and Mendeleev Ridge were extensions of the Eurasian continent, although the UN Commission said that further research was needed so the claim was neither accepted nor rejected. Russia caused further controversy in 2007 when a Russian expedition, Arktika 2007, descended to the seabed below the North Pole. The main purpose of the expedition was to collect water and soil samples that would strengthen Russia's claim to the continental shelf. However, a Russian flag was also planted on the sea floor, which did not go down particularly well with the other countries bordering the Arctic. Peter MacKay, who was the Canadian Foreign Minister, said in response, *'This isn't the 15th century. You can't go around the world and just plant flags and say, "We're claiming this territory".'*

## Consolidating your thinking

Look at the map showing the different countries' claims to the Arctic at http://www.nytimes.com/interactive/2013/12/07/sunday-review/who-owns-the-arctic.html?_r=0. On the blank map in the Teacher Book (p.18), mark on the areas of the Arctic which are claimed by each country. Do you think that this is a fair way of dividing up the area? Why do you think this?

Part of the reason that countries bordering the Arctic are so keen to extend their territories is that the area is estimated to hold the world's largest remaining unexploited gas and oil reserves. The Russian territory around the Pechora and Kara seas has already been **exploited**, supplying Russia with almost two-thirds of its oil and gas energy. However, the United States Geological Survey suggests that this area has a 50% or greater chance of having even more, as yet undiscovered, fossil fuels, which may amount to ninety billion barrels of oil and forty-seven trillion cubic metres of natural gas.

The Arctic is also home to a wide range of fish, including Arctic cod, haddock and pollock. Russia catches 600,000 tons of these fish each year, which amounts to approximately 15% of Russia's total fishing industry. Indigenous people also fish and hunt in the Arctic for subsistence. 200,000 indigenous people live in the Russian Arctic and belong to forty different groups, including the Nenets, Enets and Orok. However, as a result of increased industrial activity, climate change and **overfishing**, they are finding it increasingly difficult to survive.

Watch the special report from Channel 4 News at:

http://www.channel4.com/player/v2/player.jsp?showId=8723

Hammerfest has become the centre of the 'Cold Rush' – the rush to exploit Arctic resources. What might be the advantages and disadvantages for the town as a result?

## Consolidating your thinking

Have a look at the article at http://discovermagazine.com/2004/oct/inuit-paradox which describes a typical diet for some of the indigenous people who live in the Arctic and also how this has changed in recent years. What would you expect to eat if you went for a three course meal with indigenous people in the Arctic? How do you think your courses might change over the next century? Why do you think this? Do you think that this is a good thing?

## Additional sources of information to extend the depth and breadth of your explanation:

### Resources on the Arctic environment:

http://www.bbc.co.uk/news/world-europe-24379908

http://www.bbc.co.uk/news/world-europe-24427153

http://www.bbc.co.uk/news/world-europe-24292947

http://www.bbc.co.uk/news/world-europe-23794232

http://www.worldwildlife.org/places/arctic

http://wwf.panda.org/what_we_do/where_we_work/arctic/

### Resources on the Nenet tribe:

http://www.bbc.co.uk/tribe/tribes/nenets/

http://www.survivalinternational.org/photo-stories/3198-the-nenets-of-siberia

http://www.arcticphoto.co.uk/tundranenets.asp

http://www.theatlantic.com/infocus/2012/04/the-nenets-of-siberia/100277/

http://www.yamalpeninsulatravel.com/the-nenets/

http://www.beforethey.com/tribe/nenets

## 2.3 Can Russia exploit the Arctic sustainably?

Exploitation of resources in environmentally sensitive areas is always contentious and the exploitation of resources in the Arctic is no exception. Different groups of people have different perspectives and priorities, and may not always agree with other groups about how best to exploit the resources. Here, the question is not whether or not these resources can be exploited, or even if they should, but whether or not this can be done sustainably.

The concept of sustainability is a complicated one, but the most common definition is that it is 'development which meets the needs of the present without compromising the ability of future generations to meet their own needs' (UN Brundtland Commission). In this context, it simply means, 'Can Russia develop and exploit the resources in the Arctic so that it won't be destroyed for generations in the future?'

### ▶ Consolidating your thinking ◀

You are going to *write a speech* to bring all of this information together and help you answer the key question at the beginning of the enquiry. As highlighted, different groups of people have different perspectives and priorities and therefore may have different answers to this question. Choose one of the roles below and use the information above, plus further reading of your own (additional sources are recommended in the side boxes on these pages) to *demonstrate that you understand* that there are different perspectives on whether Russia can exploit the Arctic sustainably.

Choose one of the following roles:

- Sergei Limonov – Russian politician
- Aga Akycha – representative of the indigenous Nenet community
- Geoff Sandford – environmental activist

A sheet providing a summary for each role and questions to help you structure your speech is available for you to have a look at in the Teacher Book (pp.19–21).

Use this information and the questions on the sheet to structure a short speech which describes and explains whether you believe Russia can exploit the Arctic sustainably or not. Make sure that you explain your points clearly using factual information from the suggested sources of information.

**Resources on the Russian government's exploitation of resources:**

http://www.grida.no/files/publications/environment-times/arctic_15.pdf

http://www.gazprom.com/about/

http://www.rosneft.com/about/

http://www.theguardian.com/environment/2013/oct/02/drilling-arctic-environmental-impact-greenpeace-piracy

http://www.arcticparl.org/files/static/conf5_neelov.pdf

http://en.wikipedia.org/wiki/Fishing_industry_in_Russia

## Consolidating your thinking

Once everyone has written their speeches, get into three groups – one for each role. Working in your group you are going to vote for one speech which will be read to the rest of the class.

To do this, everyone should have an opportunity to read everyone else's speech. As you read each speech, underline one phrase in green that you think is excellent; it might contain sophisticated geographical vocabulary or figures to support the points, or might be explained in a clear way. You can also underline one phrase in red which could be improved, although you must write a comment in pencil which adds to this. For example, you could add figures or geographical vocabulary, or rephrase the explanation to make it clearer.

Once you have all had a chance to read all of the speeches, each person can have one vote for the one that they would like to represent the group (you cannot vote for your own speech!).

Having heard speeches from three different perspectives, you now need to take on the role of advisor to the Russian government. Decide upon at least three recommendations that you would make to the government which would make the exploitation of the Arctic more sustainable. You could annotate your map of the Arctic with these suggestions or write a letter to the Russian government.

Make sure you describe clearly what your recommendations are and explain why they would make exploitation more sustainable. For example, you might suggest that fishing quotas would be one of your recommendations. Would these quotas exist throughout the Arctic or only in particular places? Would it extend to all types of fish or just selected ones? How would you ensure that fishing quotas were adhered to? How would this ensure that the Arctic was exploited sustainably?

## 2.4 How can the Arctic become a sustainable tourist destination?

The Arctic is a unique environment, therefore over the last fifteen years, tourism has increased dramatically; it is estimated that currently about one million tourists visit the region each year. However, even tiny numbers of tourists can make a destination unsustainable. Consider Mount Everest, the world's highest mountain. Only about 3000 people have reached its summit since 1953, when Edmund Hillary and Tenzing Norgay conquered it for the first time.

However, as a result of advances in mountaineering equipment, it has become much easier for people with no climbing experience to ascend the mountain – provided, of course, that they have around US$80,000 for permits and guides! The tourist industry which has sprung up around **Everest Base Camp** has commercialised the area, with everything geared towards the western traveller.

> Look at the photo at:
>
> http://www.outsideonline.com/outdoor-adventure/climbing/The-Photo-that-Changed-Everest.html
>
> What do you feel when you look at this photo?

Graham Hoyland, an experienced mountaineer, has said that 'it [Mount Everest] isn't a wilderness experience – it's a McDonalds experience'. What do you think he means by this? How do you think it might be possible to prevent the same thing happening to the Arctic?

As a result of this tourism, Mount Everest was the site of *the world's highest traffic jam* when, on one day in 2012, 234 climbers queued for two and a half hours to reach the summit. It has also been termed *the world's highest rubbish dump* as oxygen cylinders, human waste and even dead bodies – which do not decompose in the sub-zero temperatures – can be found. This has become such a problem that the Nepalese government has ordered each expedition to bring 8 kg of rubbish back to Base Camp in addition to their own waste so that it can be disposed of.

*Photographer Martin Edström standing on top of a waste site along the Mount Everest trail, close to Tengboche Monastery. This is just a few hundred metres from the beaten path, but far enough for the trash not to be visible to visiting trekkers.*

## ▶ Consolidating your thinking ◀

Why might tourists want to visit the Arctic? What activities could they do whilst they are there? Look at http://www.discoveringthearctic.org.uk/5_wish_you.html which will give you some ideas. Would you like to go on holiday to the Arctic? Why? If you did decide to go, what would you need to pack?

Now imagine that you are starting your own eco-tourism company based in Anchorage, Alaska which organises holidays to the Arctic. Create a brochure which describes what tourists can do, where they will stay and, most importantly, how their holiday will be sustainable. Make sure you consider travel, energy, waste, culture and the local economy in your plans. You can find an example of an eco-tourism brochure on pages 32 and 33. There is also a code of conduct for tourism in the Arctic that you might want to adapt, which can also be found in the Teacher Book (pp.22–25). You can also have a look at https://www.travelalaska.com/ to familiarise yourself with Anchorage.

Have a look at:

http://www.ndtv.com/article/world/nepal-to-force-everest-climbers-to-collect-rubbish-490652 and http://www.bbc.co.uk/news/magazine-22680192

which suggest some of the ways in which the Nepalese government are trying to make Mount Everest a more sustainable tourist destination.

Do you think these are sensible solutions to the problems highlighted? Can you think of other solutions that would make tourism in the region more sustainable?

# DON DAENG ISLAND

- Island Walks & Bicycle Rides
- Vat Phou UNESCO World Heritage Sites
- Community Lodging

Guide to Island Communities in the Vat Phou Area

www.ecotourismlaos.com

## Do's and Don'ts

### THESE REQUESTS COME DIRECTLY FROM THE VILLAGERS

**Dress Modestly**
Please wear shirts that cover shoulders and pants or skirts that cover your knees. Shirts with a low neckline are not appropriate.

**Public Bathing:**
Please do not bathe in the nude in public. Women should cover up with a *sarong* when bathing in public.

**Photographs**
Please ask before taking close-ups or portraits. Respect those who choose not to be photographed.

**Gifts**
Please do not give anything to children as this practice encourages begging. Also, do not give medicine to anyone but a doctor or nurse.

**Body Language**
In Laos, your head is 'high' and your feet 'low' - don't gesture with your feet, and don't put your feet on furniture. Also, do not touch someone else's head. Kissing and hugging in public is impolite - please be discrete.

**Respect Local Traditions**
Please do not touch anything that may be of religious significance, such as Buddha statues, altars, and burial grounds. Please take off hats and shoes when entering temples.

**Environment**
Do not litter on land or in water; take all your garbage with you. Do not buy wildlife or wildlife products.

**Purchasing Local Crafts**
Please support local producers by purchasing newly made quality handicrafts. Do not purchase unique items such as antiques or family heirlooms that are irreplaceable.

**Drugs**
Please do not do drugs in Laos. Drug tourism does damage and sets a very bad example for Lao youth.

LNTA-ADB
Mekong Tourism Development Project

## Community Lodge & Homestays

The villagers of Ban Hua Don Daeng invite you to stay overnight in their community lodge or with local families and enjoy Southern Lao hospitality. The community lodge and village homestays were created with the support of the LNTA-ADB Mekong Tourism Development Project as an income generating project.

In order to minimize problems in the village and to make your trip more enjoyable, **advanced booking is recommended**. Contact the District Tourism Office in Champassak or the Provincial Tourism Office in Pakse (+856-031) 212 021 for more information or book in advance through a local tour company.

The community lodge has 2 common rooms each sleeping 5 people. Mattresses, pillows, blankets and mosquito nets are available. The lodge has two common bathrooms and a common dining area.

You can also stay with local families. Families can accommodate 2-4 people per household Sleeping is arranged in a common room. Homestay families have a common bathroom and provide boiled drinking water and sleeping equipment including mosquito nets.

Included in your stay is a family-style meal of Lao cuisine prepared and hosted by the villagers. Food typically includes fresh Mekong fish and locally grown organic vegetables. Vegetarian food is also available. Please order your food a couple hours in advance.

The Community Lodge on Don Daeng

Playing the *saw ee* & the *kaen*

The Community Restaurant

*Example of an eco-tourism brochure*

## Don Daeng Island

This peaceful island is located inside the Vat Phou-Champassak Heritage Landscape, a UNESCO World Heritage Site. The island is located across the Mekong River from Champassak District and offers alternative activities and community accommodation. Enjoy Don Daeng's tranquil environment and sandy beaches; visit its pre-Angkorian ruins; stay overnight in the community lodge or with local families; and learn about traditional livelihoods such as basket weaving, fishing and rice farming.

View from the island's sandy beaches

### Cultural Heritage Sites

The Don Daeng area has a rich heritage of culturally important sites, including an ancient brick stupa and collection of stone Buddha images located in the center of the island, and the ruins of Tomo Temple located just across the river. Also are the Bhuddist temples located in the villages around the island. Tours to these sites can be arranged by village guides and booked at the community lodge.

Ancient Stupa

### Tomo Temple

This monument complex is said to have been originally built as early as 7th - 8th centuries AD and later rebuilt in the 11th-12th centuries at the same time as the construction of Vat Phou. The temple is considered to be the female counterpart to the Temple of Shiva at Vat Phou, as an inscription indicates that it was dedicated to Rudrani, the shakti of Shiva (Rudra).

Tomo Temple

Example of an eco-tourism brochure

## Don Daeng Island Map

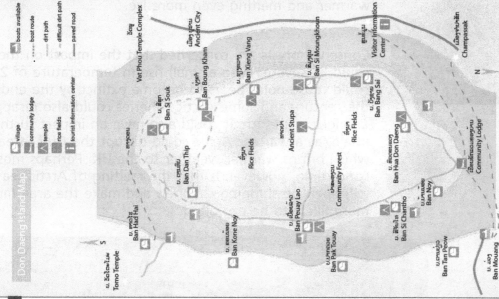

Legend:
- village
- community lodge
- temple
- rice fields
- tourist information center
- boats available
- boat route
- dirt path
- difficult dirt path
- paved road

Tomo Temple
Ban Had Hai
Ban Si Souk
Ban Dan Thip
Ban Kone Noy
Ban Peuay Lao
Ban Pak Touay
Vat Phou Temple Complex
Ancient City
Ban Boung Kham
Ban Xieng Vang
Ban Si Moungkhoun
Rice Fields
Ancient Stupa
Community Forest
Ban Bang Sai
Rice Fields
Ban Si Chantho
Ban Noy
Ban Hua Don Daeng
Community Lodge
Visitor Information Center
Champassak
Ban Tan Peow
Ban Mouang

N

**Getting to Don Daeng:** From Pakse drive south on Route 13 and turn right at Km 30. Follow the road to Ban Mouang, from where you can hire a boat across the Mekong River to Don Daeng. If you are already in Champassak District, go to the Visitor Information Center to arrange for a boat across to the island. Advance booking for the community lodge is recommended. Visit the Tourism Office in Pakse or Champassak for more information.

### Walking & Biking Around Don Daeng

Don Daeng is an ideal location for walks and bicycle rides. A country path can be followed around the island, which is shaded by a variety of trees. Along the way stop and enjoy the sweet taste of coconut or sugar cane juice and eat the fresh fruits that the island is famous for. Other sites along your walk or ride include traditional Buddhist temples, an ancient forest stupa, basket weaving villages and a protected community forest. Local guides and bicycles are available in Hua Don Daeng Village at the community lodge.

Monks on their daily alms round

### Suggested Itineraries

#### Itinerary #1:

**Day 1** - Arrive at Don Daeng in the morning. Take a locally guided tour of the island. Stay overnight in the community lodge or with homestay families.
**Day 2** - After breakfast in the village, visit Tomo Temple by boat with village guides. After returning for lunch in the village, cross the Mekong River to Champassak District and visit Vat Phou Temple Complex. Stay overnight in Champassak or return for a second night on Don Daeng.

Riding bicycles with a local guide

#### Itinerary #2:

**Day 1** - Visit Vat Phou Temple Complex in the morning and have lunch in Champassak District. In the mid-afternoon, cross the Mekong River to Don Daeng. Stay overnight in the community lodge or with homestay families.
**Day 2** - In the morning, tour the island with a local guide or visit Tomo Temple by boat. Return to Pakse or travel south to the 4,000 Islands.

*For an English-speaking guide visit the Tourism Office in Pakse or Champassak or contact a local tour company.*

Local girl making kao lum

On thin ice   33

## 2.5 How might climate change alter the Arctic?

According to scientists, the Arctic is being affected more by climate change than anywhere else in the world. Ice cover has decreased by nearly 15% since 1970 and, in 2012, the ice reached its lowest level ever recorded. The WWF estimate that, by 2080, sea ice in summer will have disappeared completely. By 2100, temperatures will be 7°C higher than temperatures during the Industrial Revolution and, as a result, sea level will have risen by at least one metre. The reason the Arctic is being so badly affected is due to the **albedo** effect. Light surfaces, like ice, reflect large amounts of heat from the sun, whilst dark surfaces, like the sea, absorb large amounts of heat from the sun. As increased temperatures melt the ice, more heat is absorbed as the surface changes from ice to sea, making the sea warmer and melting even more ice.

Conservationists are concerned that the impact on the Arctic could be severe. Even a small rise in temperature of 2°C could cause polar bears to become extinct by the end of the century and some Arctic fisheries could also disappear. Changes in the Arctic could also have an impact further afield, as a warmer Arctic could disrupt the **Gulf Stream**, which brings warmer weather to the UK. Perhaps most concerning, however, is that the melting of Arctic sea ice will open up shipping channels and make the area much more likely to be exploited.

## ► Consolidating your thinking ◄

You can read about some of the impacts of climate change in the Arctic at http://wwf.panda.org/what_we_do/where_we_work/arctic/what_we_do/climate/. Use this information to create an illustrated mind map to show the impacts of climate change on the Arctic environment.

**Arctic Ocean sea ice concentration comparison**

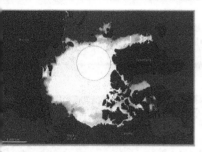 

Arctic Ocean ice coverage in September 1984

Arctic Ocean ice coverage in September 2012

Sea ice concentration (percent)

| 0 | 50 | 100 |

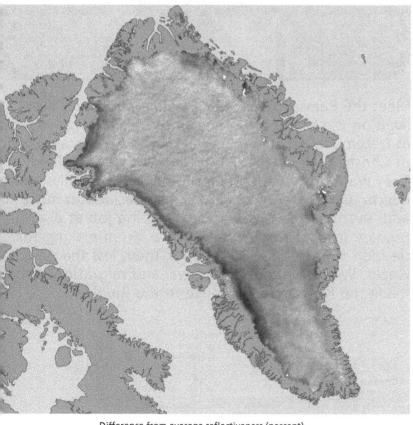

Difference from average reflectiveness (percent)

| −18 | 0 | 18 |

*Map of albedo change in Greenland. This map shows the difference between the amount of sunlight Greenland reflected in the summer of 2011 versus the average percent it reflected between 2000 and 2006.*

# 3 Welcome to Quake City, New Zealand

## How has Christchurch been affected by earthquakes?

### 3.1 Why is the Ramsay family living in the jungle?

*Damage to the area around Rangiora*

Meet the Ramsay family. Kirk, Wilma and Finn have lived on the island of Borneo since March 2012. As late as December 2011, they were living in Rangiora, outside of Christchurch on the South Island of New Zealand. They were both working locally and Kirk's family lived nearby. On 23 December 2011, they decided to move and, shortly after, Wilma got a teaching job at a primary school in Brunei on Borneo. From making the decision to moving 7800 km took them less than eight weeks. Why the sudden upheaval and **migration**? What made the Ramsay family move to the **jungle**?

People are aware they are at risk from hazard events

People want to take action to reduce risk

People can no longer accept risk

Do nothing; accept occurrence of hazards

**Stress from natural hazard events**

Absorb losses

Accept or share losses

Look for ways to reduce risk

Move locations

A person's awareness of the threat is caused by their experience of hazards and how they view the threat

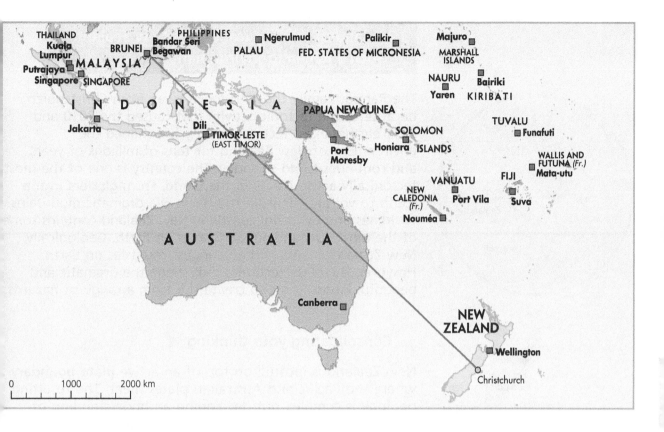

## Consolidating your thinking ◄

Look carefully at the information cards from the Teacher
Book (pp.28–29) and the images and graphs on these pages.
Your task is to draw together all these sources and develop
a written explanation that answers the question: *Why is the
Ramsay family living in the jungle?*

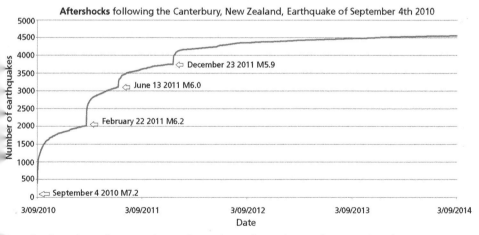

Aftershocks following the Canterbury, New Zealand, Earthquake of September 4th 2010

- December 23 2011 M5.9
- June 13 2011 M6.0
- February 22 2011 M6.2
- September 4 2010 M7.2

*Graph showing the number of earthquakes along the previously
unknown **faultline**. Note how the number declines after each big
event. There were over 3500 earthquakes in this period.*

The Ramsay family chose to move away from Christchurch because of the tectonic activity that caused the 2010 and 2011 earthquakes. Tectonic activity has shaped the environment of New Zealand for tens of millions of years and continues to do so today. The country is one of the most tectonically active places in the world. From **glaciers** in the south to volcanic fields in the north, via dramatic mountains, faultlines and beautiful coastline, New Zealand contains some of the most outstanding landscapes on Earth. Geologically, New Zealand is one of the youngest countries on Earth. However, the **plate tectonics** that shape the dramatic and beautiful landscapes also create risk from a range of **hazards**.

### ▶ Consolidating your thinking ◀

New Zealand is located on top of an active **plate boundary** where the Pacific and Australian plates meet. The resulting **geology** is complex but developing an understanding of it will help you to explain some of the dramatic landscapes and hazards that occur.

Use the images and maps on the following pages to build up a picture of the geography of New Zealand. You will need to produce your own annotated map or maps of New Zealand that show some of the interesting geographical features, as well as some of the forces at work under the surface. Use the outline map in the Teacher Book (p.30). Can you explain why New Zealand has such dramatic landscapes? You could lay maps one on top of the other, fastened on the left hand side, to create a paper **Geographical Information System (GIS)**.

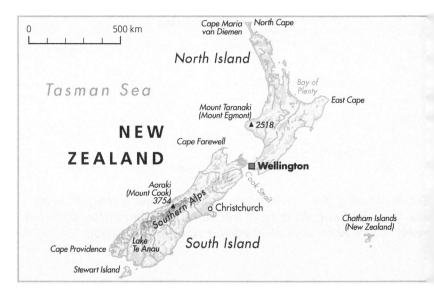

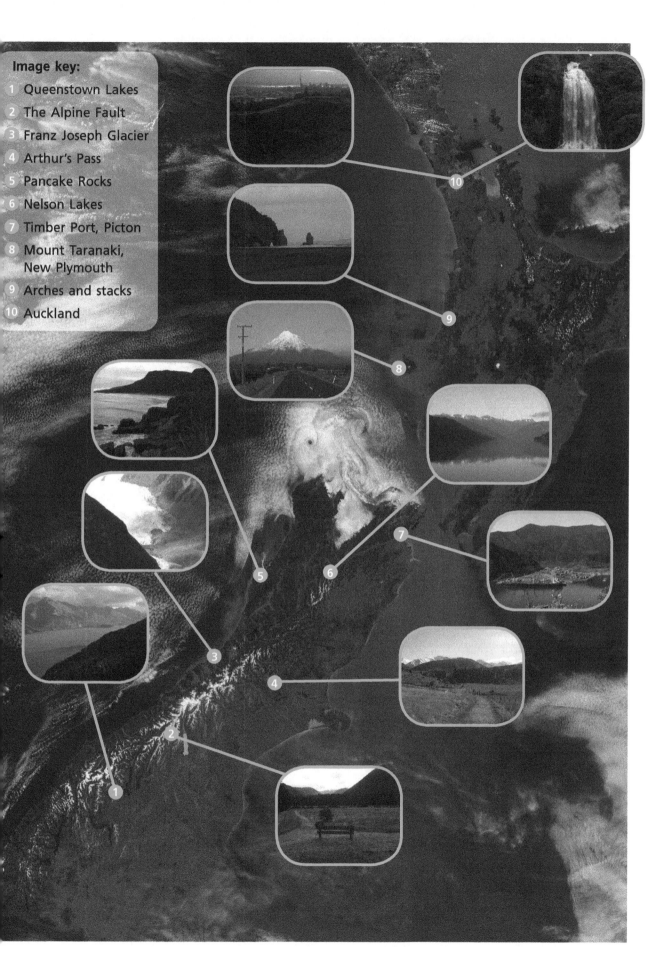

Image key:
1  Queenstown Lakes
2  The Alpine Fault
3  Franz Joseph Glacier
4  Arthur's Pass
5  Pancake Rocks
6  Nelson Lakes
7  Timber Port, Picton
8  Mount Taranaki, New Plymouth
9  Arches and stacks
10 Auckland

## Plate boundaries

### Constructive boundary

Can lead to small earthquakes
and volcanic activity

### Destructive boundary

Can lead to volcanoes, earthquakes
and risk of tsunamis

### Conservative boundary

Can lead to significant earthquakes

*The complex plate boundaries under New Zealand*

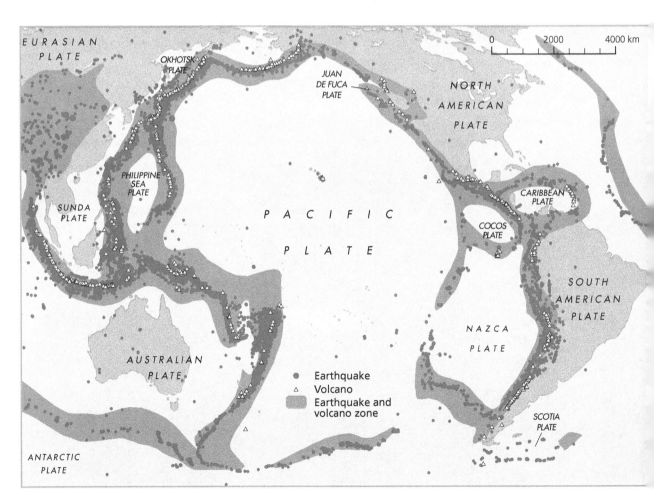

The volcano map shows areas of volcanic activity, not just individual volcanoes. For example, the Auckland Volcanic Field is made up of over fifty separate volcanoes scattered across New Zealand's largest city!

Questions to consider:

• What is the pattern of volcanic activity in New Zealand?

• How does the information on pages 38 to 40 help to explain this pattern?

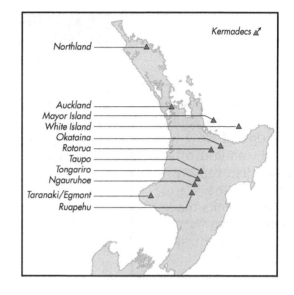

This map shows all the earthquakes in New Zealand over the past ten years at a depth of 40 km or below. Very deep earthquakes are less likely to cause surface damage and some of these will not even have been felt by humans. There is a very clear pattern under the North Island and there are very few deep earthquakes under the South Island.

Questions to consider:

• What is the pattern of deep earthquakes in New Zealand?

• How does this map link to the plate boundary information on page 40?

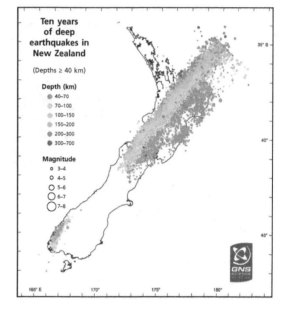

The shallow earthquake map shows data for the past ten years. There are large concentrations of earthquakes along fault lines. Many of the magnitude 4 and upwards earthquakes could have been felt by humans.

Questions to consider:

• What is the pattern of shallow earthquakes in New Zealand?

How does this differ from the deep earthquake map?

Can you suggest reasons for the pattern?

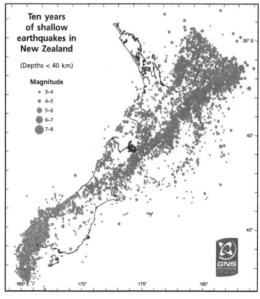

Working with a partner and drawing on your knowledge of New Zealand, can you offer four detailed reasons to explain why there are shops and banks made from shipping containers in central Christchurch?

The images on this page were taken in the **central business district (CBD)** of Christchurch on the South Island of New Zealand. This is a busy city of nearly 380,000 people, yet in 2014 the CBD is dominated by shipping container shops, empty spaces, cranes and construction work. Why?

Of course, you will know that the simple explanation is that Christchurch suffered two earthquakes in 2010 and 2011, but the reasons for the use of shipping containers as shops are more complex than 'there was an earthquake'.

The shipping container mall is known as the Re:start Mall and is part of the earthquake recovery strategy in Christchurch. Question 3.3 will give you the opportunity to investigate the two earthquakes and to examine in detail how the city is recovering.

## ▶ Consolidating your thinking ◀

You will need to work individually using the information and factfiles on pages 45 to 47 and the framework from the Teacher Book (p.33) to investigate, compare, contrast and establish the link between the September 2010 and February 2011 earthquakes.

Following this, you should draw upon the information about the recovery plans on pages 48 and 49, plus your own research, to produce a short video or presentation in the style of a news report that demonstrates your knowledge and understanding of:

• The tectonic setting of Christchurch (why they have earthquakes here).

• The 2010 and 2011 earthquakes (what happened).

• The effects of the earthquakes on:

  o People – the Ramsay family, for example (social), see http://www.quakestories.govt.nz/stories

  o **Infrastructure**, jobs and companies (economic)

  o The land, rivers and surrounding hills (environmental)

The steps taken to recover and redevelop central Christchurch.

Christchurch today and plans for the future. What are the **residential red zones** and what should be done with them?

> You could use iMovie, Movie Maker, PowerPoint, Prezi or emaze to show your understanding. This could be completed in small groups with different roles assigned – studio presenter, reporter, geology expert, script writer, image researcher, ICT expert and director, for example.

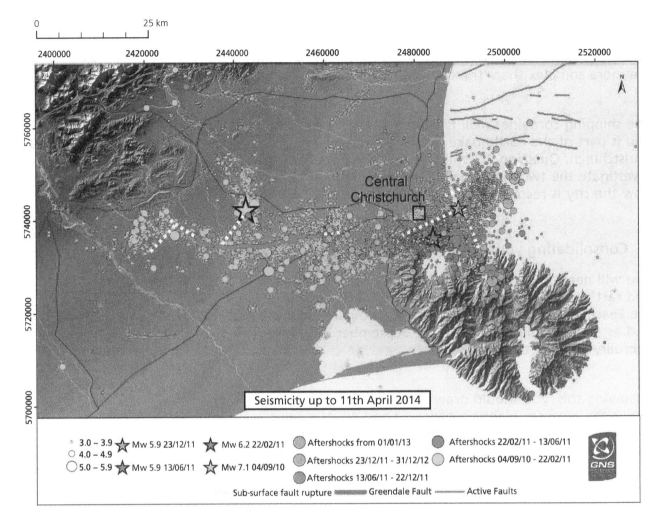

Scale: 0 — 25 km

Top axis labels: 2400000  2420000  2440000  2460000  2480000  2500000  2520000

Left axis labels: 5760000  5740000  5720000  5700000

Central Christchurch

Seismicity up to 11th April 2014

Legend:
- 3.0 – 3.9
- 4.0 – 4.9
- 5.0 – 5.9
- ⭐ Mw 5.9 23/12/11
- ⭐ Mw 5.9 13/06/11
- ⭐ Mw 6.2 22/02/11
- ⭐ Mw 7.1 04/09/10
- Aftershocks from 01/01/13
- Aftershocks 23/12/11 - 31/12/12
- Aftershocks 13/06/11 - 22/12/11
- Aftershocks 22/02/11 - 13/06/11
- Aftershocks 04/09/10 - 22/02/11
- Sub-surface fault rupture ▬▬▬ Greendale Fault ——— Active Faults

GNS SCIENCE

## 3.4 Why is this region prone to earthquakes?

As we have already discovered, New Zealand sits on a plate boundary with complex geology – a destructive plate boundary to the north, with subduction and volcanoes, and a transform or side by side boundary under the south. The movement of the Australian and Pacific Plates subject New Zealand to tremendous forces.

This builds up stress in the rocks around Christchurch until they reach breaking point and suddenly rupture along weaknesses called faults. The energy is released in seismic shockwaves that travel outwards – an earthquake. Often, not all the stress is released in one go and more movement occurs as the rocks find their new position. These smaller movements are aftershocks and they will reduce over time.

# The 2010 Darfield Earthquake
## 4 September 2010

### The Richter Scale

| 0 | 1 | 2 | 3 | 4 | 5 | 6 | 7 | 8 | 9 |
|---|---|---|---|---|---|---|---|---|---|
| Unfelt | Minor | Small | Moderate | Moderate | Strong | Strong | Major | Major | Great |

**04:35** local time

**7.1** on the Richter Scale

Depth of **10.46 km**

↔ **45 km**
fault rupture length

**40 seconds**
duration, and was felt across the South Island and the lower third of the North Island

**671 kilo tonnes**
energy release of TNT equivalent

Epicentre: a previously unknown section of the Greendale Fault

**8 km** southeast of Darfield &
**37.9 km** west of central Christchurch

**100**
injured people

widespread damage to infrastructure and housing

disruption to many businesses

- Across the region there was widespread damage to infrastructure and housing and disruption to many businesses. A state of emergency was declared.

- Despite the tremendous damage and the constant aftershocks that made life very challenging, many people felt lucky that there was no loss of life.

- Railway lines buckled and had to be repaired

- Soil **liquefaction** caused a lot of problems with flooding damaging buried pipes and building foundations.

- Because this earthquake happened at night, when most people were in their beds, there were not many people injured by falling buildings or **landslides**.

- Two people were seriously injured, with approximately 100 total injuries.

# The 2011 Christchurch Earthquake
22 February 2011

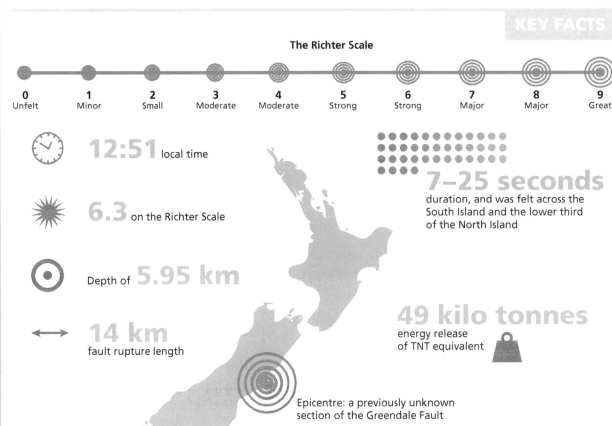

**The Richter Scale**

| 0 | 1 | 2 | 3 | 4 | 5 | 6 | 7 | 8 | 9 |
|---|---|---|---|---|---|---|---|---|---|
| Unfelt | Minor | Small | Moderate | Moderate | Strong | Strong | Major | Major | Great |

**12:51** local time

**6.3** on the Richter Scale

Depth of **5.95 km**

**14 km**
fault rupture length

**7–25 seconds**
duration, and was felt across the
South Island and the lower third
of the North Island

**49 kilo tonnes**
energy release
of TNT equivalent

Epicentre: a previously unknown
section of the Greendale Fault

**6.7 km** southeast of central Christchurch

**185**
deaths

**7000**
injured people

**100,000**
damaged buildings

- 185 people died across the city and nearly 7000 were injured.

- This much shallower earthquake was on a fault that was angled right at central Christchurch.

- **Seismologists** believe this earthquake was triggered by strain build-up from the September earthquake.

- The shallow depth meant little of the energy was lost before reaching the surface.

- Christchurch was subjected to intense shaking with widespread devastation to buildings, homes and infrastructure.

- Buildings weakened by the 2010 earthquake collapsed. Up to 100,000 were damaged.

- The CBD suffered significant destruction and the iconic cathedral spire collapsed.

- 80% of the city lost power.

- The Canterbury TV building suffered a catastrophic collapse and fire, causing 115 of the 185 deaths.

- Large rockfalls caused further damage in the hills around the city.

- East Christchurch suffered very badly from liquefaction as it was built on a drained swamp.

- Large parts of Christchurch suffered from liquefaction where water and silt were squeezed upwards through the soil. Roads and parks flooded, houses sunk and sewage pipes cracked.

- Urban search and rescue teams were rescuing people within one hour of the earthquake and international teams arrived within twenty-four hours.

## 3.5 How does a city recover from an earthquake?

*Christchurch Cathedral in 2014*

Once the dust has settled and the global news crews have finished reporting on the human cost and rising death tolls and moved onto the next big story – which in this case was the March 2011 Japanese earthquake and **tsunami** – how does a city begin the complex process of recovery from a disaster like this?

With the Christchurch earthquakes, the key phases of response to the disasters were:

- The immediate search and rescue operation – hours and days following the earthquake.

- The demolish, repair, patch up and planning phase – September 2010 to December 2011.

- Begin to rebuild, replace and reconstruct – 2012 to 2014.

- Construct, restore and improve – 2015 to 2020 and beyond

The complex and comprehensive recovery plan has been put into place by organisations set up by the New Zealand Government. They created **CERA (Canterbury Earthquake Recovery Authority)** and appointed an earthquake minister to the government.

CERA are managing the recovery and rebuild strategy. For Christchurch this has meant decisions have had to be made on the following factors:

- How to manage the lack of sewerage, water and power across the city.

- What to demolish and rebuild in the CBD red zone (closed off for safety).

- How to manage the insurance claiming process.

- How to rebuild the economy.

- What transport networks needed to be repaired or replaced.

- Which houses can be repaired or demolished across the city.

- What to do with the land that suffered liquefaction.

Nothing has changed for this shop since it was cleared on 25 February 2011

Some buildings are still awaiting demolition

Turning these decisions into action has been extremely challenging for Christchurch – especially with big aftershocks causing more damage. For example, CERA had to decide which homes to buy from owners, on land so badly damaged by liquefaction that it is unsafe to build on. Over 7300 homes have been purchased and this 630 hectare area of land, known as the residential red zone, is currently abandoned. Plans for its future are undecided.

## ▶ Consolidating your thinking ◀

Your final task in this enquiry is to develop a plan for these zones and then to submit these ideas to CERA as part of their consultation. They will accept suggestions from all around the world, so this is your opportunity to contribute to the recovery of Christchurch. They will welcome presentations, videos, images and documents.

You can choose to submit your plans to CERA as part of their strategy for this area. Use the extra guidance for what Christchurch needs in these zones from the Teacher Book (pp.34–35).

As part of your video you will need to research the recovery plan in general and then make considered suggestions on what to do with the residential red zone in Christchurch.

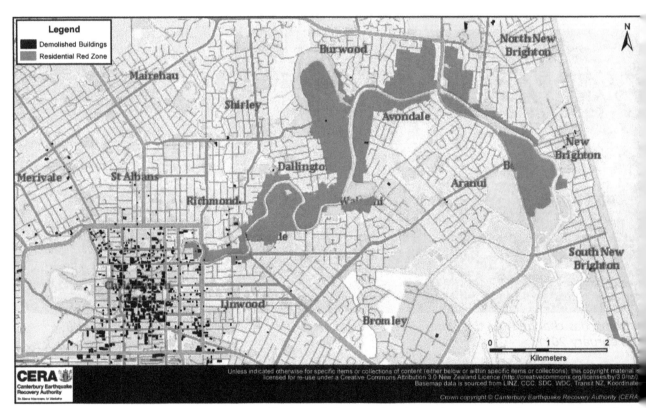

*This map shows demolished buildings in black and the residential red zones which cannot be built upon*

Use the resources from this enquiry and the hyperlinks below to explore the recovery strategy by following these steps:

- Visit the CERA website: http://cera.govt.nz/

- Read some of the Greater Canterbury recovery updates: http://cera.govt.nz/news?tid[]=277

- Explore GIS maps of the earthquake damage: http://maps.cera.govt.nz/html5/?viewer=public

- Explore the key CBD rebuild projects: http://www.futurechristchurch.co.nz/central-city

- Visit http://ccdu.govt.nz/ to watch the video on the redevelopment of the CBD and to explore in detail the plans.

- Download the CCDU AR app from the app/play store and use with the map at: http://ccdu.govt.nz/sites/default/files/ christchurch-central-anchor-projects-and-precincts-map-a4-2014-07-18.pdf for an augmented reality view of the redevelopment.

- Examine the impact of the earthquakes on population and the economy: http://www.stats.govt.nz/Census/2013-census/profile-and-summary-reports/2013-census-infographic-chch.aspx

- Use http://file.stuff.co.nz/thepress/zonelife/ to explore the residential red zone through maps, images and video.

Once your plans are complete for the red zone you can upload them at https://canvasredzone.org.nz/. This is a fantastic opportunity to show your geographical creativity and to make a valuable contribution to the recovery of Christchurch from the devastating earthquakes of 2010 and 2011.

You could also look to other cities for inspiration, for example Berlin had a 600 hectare space to fill when it closed an airport – see http://www.tempelhoferfreiheit.de/en/.

If you would like to see some ideas in action, then explore

http://www.gapfiller.org.nz/

to see how creative use is being made of the gaps that exist all over Christchurch.
▶▶

# 4 Managing the coast

## When is doing nothing actually doing something?

Measuring 12,429 km, the United Kingdom has the twelfth longest coastline of any country in the world – greater than either Brazil or India. Nowhere in the UK is further than 113 km from the coast and three million people (5% of the UK population) live in its **coastal margins**.

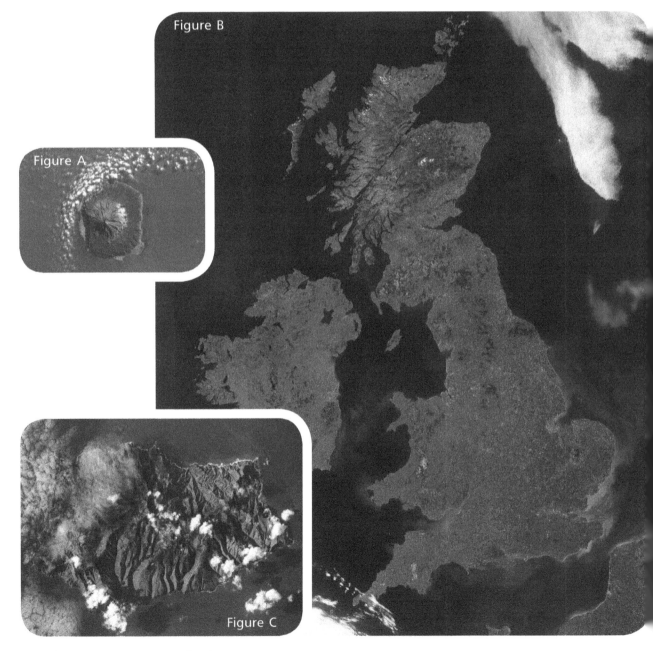

Figure B

Figure A

Figure C

## 4.1 What is an island?

You would be right, up to a point, in saying that an **island** is any area of land surrounded by water, but geographers recognise two types of islands in the world as you will discover on page 54.

Working with a partner and using an atlas or wall map of the world, identify the islands A to H which appear on these pages. The islands are: **Tasmania**; **Borneo**; **Baffin Island**; **Great Britain**; **Tristan da Cunha**; **Iceland** and **Saint Helena**. Once you have named and located them, divide them into two sets of four. You will need to agree a rationale (a set of reasons or a logical basis for a course of action) for your decision and share it with the rest of the group, for example size, shape, location etc.

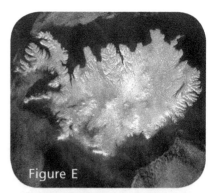
Figure E

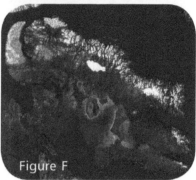
Figure F

Figure D

Figure G

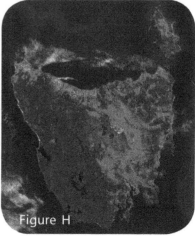
Figure H

## 4.2 How do *continental* and *oceanic* islands differ?

Most of the largest islands in the world are classified as *continental islands,* which mean that they lie on the **continental shelf** of a continent. This is the submerged border of a continent that slopes gradually out into the ocean before reaching a point (the *continental slope*) where it drops steeply to the ocean bottom.

Oceanic islands do not sit on a continental shelf and most are created by tectonic activity such as at **subduction zones,** where two plates carrying oceanic crust converge. When one of these plates plunges down beneath the other, the crust that it is carrying melts, creating **magma,** which rises up to form a line of volcanic islands above the ocean known as **island arcs**.

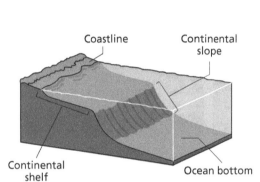

*Diagram of the continental shelf*

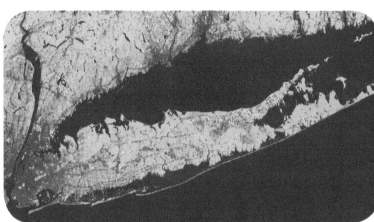

*A continental island: Long Island, New York State, USA*

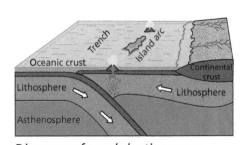

*Diagram of a subduction zone*

*An oceanic island: Mount Cleveland in the Aleutian Islands of Alaska*

## ▶ Consolidating your thinking ◀

Tamu Massif, the largest single volcano on Earth, is in fact located below the sea and remained undiscovered for 145 million years. Read through the article in *National Geographic* at http://news.nationalgeographic.com/news/2013/09/130905-tamu-massif-shatsky-rise-largest-volcano-oceanography-science/ which describes its recent discovery and main physical features.

Tamu Massif is a **shield volcano**. Using the resources at http://www.bbc.co.uk/schools/gcsebitesize/geography/natural_hazards/volcanoes_rev3.shtml produce an annotated diagram to describe and explain the main features of a shield volcano.

New volcanic oceanic islands occur quite regularly in some parts of the world. One such area is the Ogasawara island chain off the southeast coast of Japan. A recent arrival here is documented at http://www.dailymail.co.uk/sciencetech/article-2511115/Volcanic-eruption-Pacific-Ocean-creates-new-island-coast-Japan.html. All of the islands of Ogasawara form part of what geographers call the **Pacific Ring of Fire**.

Using the information at http://geography.about.com/cs/earthquakes/a/ringoffire.htm explain why it is that 75% of the world's active volcanoes are found along the Pacific Ring of Fire.

**The Ogasawara island chain**

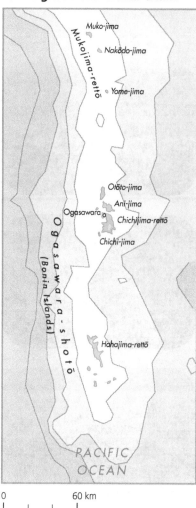

0    60 km

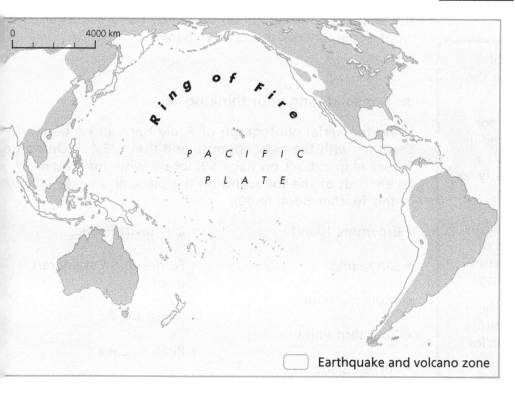

Earthquake and volcano zone

Brownsea Island, which is situated in one of the world's largest natural **harbours** at Poole along the south coast of England, is remarkable for several things. One of these special things is that until about 9000 years ago it wasn't an island at all but a hill, surrounded by mostly dry land. Why do you think it's an island today?

Working with a partner, divide an A3 sheet of plain paper (landscape) into two halves with a pencil line, from top to bottom. At the top of the left hand side write the title: *Brownsea Hill during the Ice Age* and on the top of the right hand side write the title: *Brownsea Island at the end of the Ice Age.* In the Teacher Book (p.39) there are descriptions of Brownsea at these two times. Each of you needs to take a turn reading a description and drawing a sketch. From the description which will be read to you, draw a sketch of *Brownsea Hill during the Ice Age* and then alternate so that your partner sketches *Brownsea Island at the end of the Ice Age* from the description you read out.

Areas of low lying river **valleys** that were submerged by rising sea levels at the end of the last Ice Age to form coastal inlets or **bays**, such as Poole Harbour, are called **rias.** In these inlets the old hilltops (such as Brownsea) stick up above the surface of the water to form islands. Changes to the landscape such as these, caused by rising sea levels, are what geographers call **eustatic change**.

What is the area of Brownsea Island to the nearest km²?

The main channel for ships in Poole Harbour is shallow and has to be dredged regularly to maintain its depth. What is the other challenge presented by the physical shape of the harbour for vessels entering and leaving?

What evidence is there on the map to indicate use of the harbour for leisure?

### ▶ Consolidating your thinking ◀

Using the aerial photograph of Poole Harbour on page 57, together with the map opposite and the 1:25 000 Ordnance Survey map extract on page 59, locate with annotated labels each of the following on the black and white image in the Teacher Book (p.40):

- Brownsea Island
- Sandbanks
- Poole Harbour
- Goathorn Point
- Furzey Island

- Old Town Poole
- Ferries and Catamaran quay
- Parkstone Bay
- Boating Lake

An aerial photograph of Poole Harbour

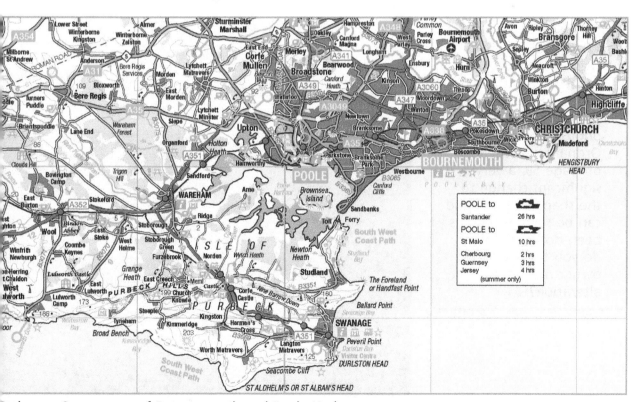

Ordnance Survey map of Bournemouth and Poole Harbour area

Using all four images of Brownsea Island, consider the following:

- In 1586, what important function does the map suggest Brownsea Island had at that time?

- What evidence is there on this map to suggest that Poole was already an important port and how the surrounding countryside was being used?

- By 1780, a much more accurate map of Brownsea shows how the owner was using some of the island – how was it being used?

- When comparing the 1780 map and the Ordnance Survey map of 1812 from the Teacher Book with the modern aerial photograph and Ordnance Survey map on page 59, a very significant change to the shape of the island can be seen. What has been done and why do you think the owner made this alteration?

During the past 500 years or so, the physical shape of Brownsea Island has changed. The oldest surviving map of the entrance to Poole Harbour showing Brownsea Island (labelled as *Brunekley*) was produced by Treswell in 1586 (this is available in the Teacher Book on page 41). The map below originates from 1780. By 1812, the first Ordnance Survey map of Poole Harbour had been created (a copy is available in the Teacher Book on page 41). The aerial photograph on this page shows the island today.

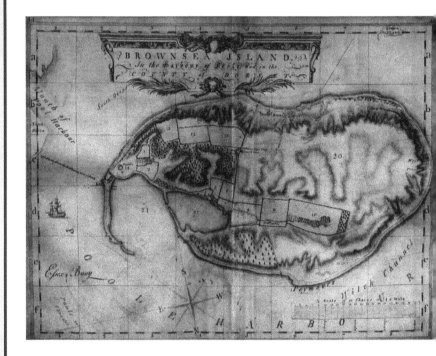

## 4.5 What was the reclaimed land of St Mary's Bay used for?

During the 1850s, the owner of Brownsea Island, Colonel Waugh, built a shingle and brick wall around what was then called St Mary's Bay (marked as 21 on the 1780 map on page 58) and is today referred to on the modern OS map as *Brownsea Road*, although it is not a road but a sea wall. After building the sea wall, the next thing he did was install a wind pump to drain the water out of the bay into Poole Harbour to create dry land. Geographers call the kind of land made by draining areas of sea water **reclaimed land**. In time, the enclosed reclaimed land of St Mary's Bay became dry enough to be used for farming.

▶ **Consolidating your thinking** ◀

- In the Teacher Book (p.42) there is a copy of an extract of the Brownsea Island farm estate records for 1857, which shows how the newly reclaimed land was used. The newly reclaimed land of St Mary's Bay added eighty-eight acres (thirty-five hectares) to the Brownsea Island farm estate. By what percentage did the land area of the estate increase?

- What is **pasture**? What are oats and what is the link between growing this crop and the pasture land? What does **fallow** mean? Why was it necessary to leave fields fallow in the nineteenth century and why is it much less common on British farms today? Along with oats, barley and mangelwurzels (wurzels) were also grown then as **fodder crops**. What are fodder crops?

- You will see from the modern photographs of Brownsea Island on this page that the reclaimed land inside the sea wall is no longer dry and used for farmland. What is it like today? Why do you think that the land is once again flooded? There are clues in the photographs (look particularly at the level of sea water in Poole Harbour compared with the level of water inside the sea wall). There are also clues on the OS map of Brownsea Island on page 59. What is happening to the water draining out of West Lake and East Lake?

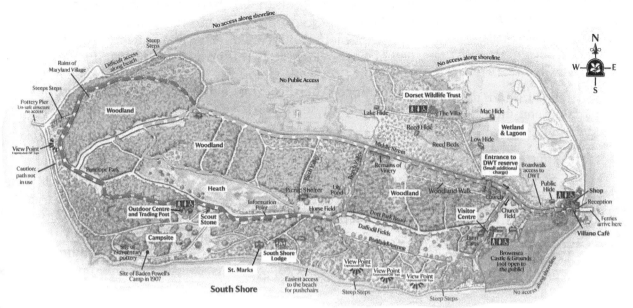

*Modern interpretation map of Brownsea Island*

## 4.6 Why is the lagoon on Brownsea Island so important?

As can be seen on the interpretation map of Brownsea Island above, St Mary's Bay is now a **lagoon**. The land that was once reclaimed and used for farming is now open water with scattered mud banks

St Mary's Bay has filled up with open water to create a lagoon for two reasons. Firstly, fresh water from East Lake and West Lake in the centre of the island is draining into the lagoon behind the sea wall. Secondly, the old sea wall that was built around St Mary's Bay is now leaking. Salt water from Poole Harbour is passing through the sea wall to mix with fresh water in the lagoon to create what is known as **brackish** water. This lagoon of brackish water is today incredibly important as a wildlife **habitat**. The lagoon has been designated as a **Ramsar site**, a **Special Protection Area (SPA)** and a **Site of Special Scientific Interest (SSSI)**. Over 100 hectares of the island, including the lagoon, has been leased to Dorset Wildlife Trust, which manages the site for wildlife.

### ▶ Consolidating your thinking ◀

What does being a Ramsar site, SPA and SSSI mean? Look at the interpretation map of Brownsea Island and the photographs on this page. What has Dorset Wildlife Trust done on the reserve to make the area accessible to visitors and to encourage resident and visiting birds?

Take a look at the Dorset Wildlife Trust lagoon webcam at:

http://www.dorsetwildlifetrust.org.uk/brownsea_island_nature_reserve.html

Describe the landscape that you can see. What do you feel is 'natural' and what has been created by humans?

In the Teacher Book (p.43) there is an extract from the *Birds of Poole Harbour* website at http://www.birdsofpooleharbour.co.uk/brownsea-webcam called 'What am I watching?' The populations of six types of birds found at Brownsea Island are of international or national importance. These can be seen below. Produce a profile of each of these six birds to include:

- General description

- Photograph

- Food requirements

- Population number in the UK

- Song

- Distribution in the UK (use the outline map in the Teacher Book on page 77)

- Status – red, amber or green and what this means

You can begin your research at http://www.rspb.org.uk/wildlife/birdguide/.

## 4.7 How is the coastline of Brownsea Island changing?

In 1962, the *National Trust* became the new owners of Brownsea Island. The National Trust is one of the largest charities and land owners in the UK. It operates as a conservation organisation and owns many beauty spots and heritage properties, such as historic houses and gardens. Today, the coastline of Brownsea Island is presenting a real challenge to the National Trust.

### ▶ Consolidating your thinking ◀

Look at the photographs below of different parts of the coastline of Brownsea Island. What do they show happening? Using the modern OS map on page 59, can you suggest different places around the coastline of Brownsea where the photographs might have been taken? What do you think might be causing these changes? Given that 150,000 visitors come to Brownsea Island every year, why do you think these changes are creating a challenge for the National Trust?

The geology or rock structure of Brownsea Island is fairly simple as shown in the diagram below. On the surface there is a shallow layer of gravels called **Pleistocene gravels** in which plants and trees grow. Below the gravels is a thicker layer of sand known as **Branksome sands** and then finally a third layer of **Parkstone clay**.

**The geology of Brownsea Island**

Vegetation
Pleistocene gravels
Branksome sands
Parkstone clay

Vegetation
Pleistocene gravels
Branksome sands
Parkstone clay

## ▶ Consolidating your thinking ◀

Now compare your diagram with the annotated sketch of cliff erosion in the Teacher Book (p.44). Add the same labels used in this sketch to your diagram.

Along the south coast of Brownsea Island very serious erosion is occurring to the cliffs, as can be seen in the photographs on the previous page. The following is an extract from *Living with a Changing Coastline* by the Environment Agency which describes what is happening along Brownsea Island's south coast. Using this description, draw a diagram or sketch with labels to show visually what is happening here.

'Two processes of erosion are in operation along the south coast of Brownsea. Firstly, waves approaching the island from the south wear away hollows and caves at the base of the cliffs, causing an overhang to form. Because this overhang is unsupported it eventually collapses down onto the beach. Secondly, rain water quickly drains through the gravels and sand (which are both impermeable – i.e. allow water to pass through them) – until it meets the clay layer (which is impermeable and will not allow water to pass through it). When the percolating rainwater reaches the lower layer of clay (which is impermeable) it flows out as a spring or stream. This makes the sand above very unstable by creating a slippery layer between it and the clay below. As a result the sand slumps or slips down onto the shore.'

For the ferries bringing 150,000 visitors a year, the pier on the east coast is the only access point on the island. In addition, people live in the properties close to the sea and the National Trust (the owner of the island) has its offices, shops and café here as well. In the short term, the National Trust has positioned temporary flood barriers to counter the risk of flooding over the next few years but this will not offer a longer, more **sustainable** solution to the problem.

Along the southeast coastline of Brownsea Island another problem has arisen. When southerly storms combine with high tides in the harbour the piers and properties along the coast are flooded. These are shown in the photographs below. ▶▶

The lagoon in the northeast of the island presents a third coastal management challenge to the National Trust. Here, a decision is going to have to be made as to what should be done with the sea wall surrounding the lagoon. Now over 150 years old, the sea wall, made of earth and brick, is disintegrating. This is allowing salt water from Poole Harbour to seep into the lagoon.

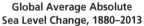

**Global Average Absolute Sea Level Change, 1880–2013**

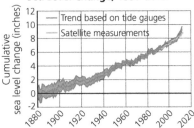

The coastline of Britain is incredibly important for lots of reasons. People live on and close to the coast and millions earn a living from activities associated with it such as fishing, **tourism**, power generation, **trade** and **transport**. In addition to human beings, the British coastline is also home to a very wide range of plants and wildlife that live in and on its different habitats such as marshes, mudflats and cliffs. Some parts of the coastline are under attack and are being worn away through the natural process of erosion, whilst in other places new land is building up as eroded material is deposited through longshore drift.

All of these conflicting things inevitably lead to pressure building up on some sections of coast. For example, should a new hotel be built that will create new jobs and much needed income for local people on sand dunes that are the home of sand lizards, one of the UK's rarest invertebrates? When pressure such as this occurs, decisions have to be made as to what is the most sustainable option for the future. Considering the costs and benefits of different alternatives as to how the coast might be used and ultimately recommending the 'best' way forward is what geographers refer to as **coastal management**. This is what the National Trust is having to do on Brownsea Island.

> ► **Consolidating your thinking** ◄

For the remainder of this century, managing the coastline of Britain is going to be an increasing challenge for geographers. Study the data on this page. What are the added problems going to be?

**Global warming 1910–2010**

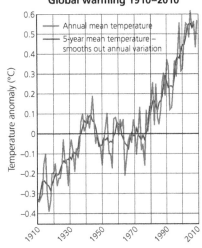

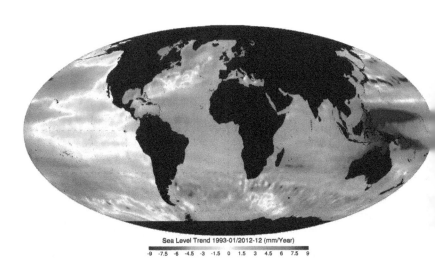

Sea Level Trend 1993-01/2012-12 (mm/Year)

-9   -7.5   -6   -4.5   -3   -1.5   0   1.5   3   4.5   6   7.5   9

## 4.9 When it comes to coastal change, what are the main management options?

When it comes to deciding on what should be done about coastal areas such as Brownsea Island that are being affected by erosion and flooding by the sea, there are three main options known as:

- **Hold the line**

- **Managed realignment**

- **No active intervention**

▶ **Consolidating your thinking** ◀

Working with a partner or small group, discuss each of these terms and agree on what you think each might involve doing (or not doing). The images below all link with the three management strategies and will help with your thinking and reasoning.

Watch the film
*Brownsea Island
Shoreline Restoration
Project* at: http://www.
youtube.com/watch?v=
ifDGs_eAIZ8

What is the National Trust's policy on the cliffs along the south coast of Brownsea?

What did the National Trust have to do before it could allow natural coastal processes to take priority?

When it comes to this coastline, what do you understand by the term *'doing nothing is actually doing something'*?

▶▶

In relation to managing the coast, the National Trust says:

- *We will work with natural processes wherever possible, taking a long term view.*

- *Interference in natural processes will only be supported for reasons of overriding benefit to society.*

- *Valued natural and coastal heritage features will be conserved as far as possible.*

*See: Shifting Shores*
(http://www.national
trust.org.uk/document-
1355834809529)

▶▶

## 4.10 Which coastal management option has the National Trust decided upon for Brownsea Island?

Faced with increasing challenges associated with global warming and **climate change** in the next 100 years, such as sea level rise (as much as one metre in Poole Harbour) and more frequent southerly winter storms, the National Trust has already made two important decisions about how the coastline of the south and southeast of Brownsea Island should be managed in the future.

Along the southeast coast a flood barrier to protect the pier and coastal properties has been put in as a temporary measure to **hold the line** here for a while. But the landing pier and the properties associated with it are too important to the island to abandon to the sea. The houses, offices, shops and café will all be rebuilt further inland with the existing buildings being demolished, so **managed realignment** of the coast will be employed here in the long term.

## 4.11 What is the best option for Brownsea lagoon?

A new landing pier much more **resilient** to the changes which are likely as a result of climate change will need to be designed and constructed in much the same position as the existing one. On a piece of A3 paper, design a new pier for Brownsea Island that meets the following brief:

- Can cope with up to 200,000 visitors passing through each year, with twelve ferry landings and departures a day in the busiest summer months.

- Allows visitors to move easily and safely from the pier to the National Trust shops and café which will have been relocated inland.

- Is constructed from sustainable and environmentally friendly raw materials and integrates well with existing buildings.

- Can cope with rising sea levels within Poole Harbour in the future as well as more frequent southerly winter storms which from time to time might coincide with tidal surges.

You have been asked to advise the National Trust on how to manage Brownsea lagoon in the future. Draft a letter to persuade the National Trust to follow the course of action that you recommend. In preparation for this you will need to consider the following opinions and decide upon which you feel should take priority:

1 Some people and organisations argue that since the lagoon is today part of the Poole Harbour Ramsar site, it must be preserved at all costs by both raising the height of the sea wall and making it completely water tight. There are less than 2000 Ramsar sites in the world and the British government is internationally bound by law to protect the lagoon as a wetland habitat of great 'natural heritage' and importance for wading birds.

2 Others feel that although the lagoon provides an important wildlife habitat today, it has only been like it is for a short time (about 150 years) and is entirely man-made. For thousands of years before this the lagoon was open sea water. It is only like it is today because humans built a sea wall around the bay to reclaim the land for farming during Victorian times. What is happening now, they say, is a natural process of the sea reclaiming what it once possessed. They argue strongly that the National Trust should be true to its stated principles of taking a long-term view when it comes to coastal management and not interfering with natural processes. This pressure group feels that conserving the birdlife of the lagoon is not 'an overriding benefit to society' since the birds can move to other, similar habitats in Poole Harbour.

In drafting your letter to the National Trust manager of Brownsea Island it will be important for you to draw on the conventions of persuasive writing so that what you are saying has maximum impact. When you are writing to persuade, your aim is to make your reader agree with a point of view or convince them of the need to follow advice or take action. To achieve this there are a variety of literary techniques you can utilise. In the Teacher Book (p.45) there is an example of a letter arguing the case for greater freedom when it comes to genetic engineering. Read this through in conjunction with the text, sentence and word level conventions sheet, also in the Teacher Book (p.46), to familiarise yourself with how you might go about structuring your letter.

**Additional support is available at:**

www.lancsngfl.ac.uk/ nationalstrategy/ks3/english/ getfile.php?src=446/ Argue+Persuade+KS3.doc

and

http://www.bbc.co.uk/schools/ gcsebitesize/english/writing/ writingtoarguerev4.shtml

where there is another example of a persuasive letter, this time arguing against school uniforms. The most important thing to remember as you draft your letter is that its purpose is to influence the readers' view and to change minds. ◀◀

# 5 Life's a beach!

## Why do most Australians live on the edge?

Australia is the sixth-largest country in the world by land area (about the same size as the United States without including Alaska) but with just twenty-four million inhabitants it ranks down at fifty-first position in terms of population size. Consequently, its **population density** is very low at an average of 2.9 people per km². Only Mongolia, Western Sahara, Suriname, Mauritania and Botswana have fewer people per km².

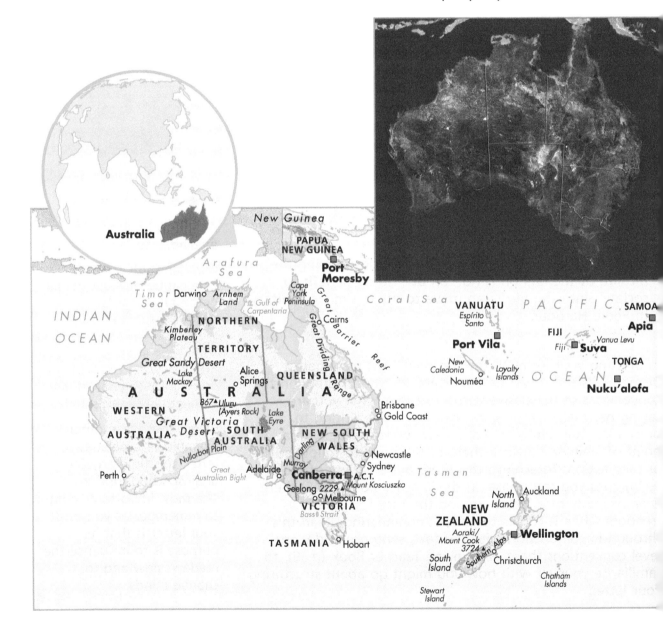

**Australia: Population Data**

| State/territory | Land area (km²) | Population (2011 census) | Population density (per km²) | % of population in capital |
|---|---|---|---|---|
| Australian Capital Territory | 2358 | 357,222 | 151.49 | 99.6% |
| New South Wales | 800,642 | 6,917,658 | 8.64 | 63% |
| Victoria | 227,416 | 5,354,042 | 23.54 | 71% |
| Queensland | 1,730,648 | 4,332,739 | 2.50 | 46% |
| South Australia | 983,482 | 1,596,572 | 1.62 | 73.5% |
| Western Australia | 2,529,875 | 2,239,170 | 0.89 | 73.4% |
| Tasmania | 68,401 | 495,354 | 7.24 | 41% |
| Northern Territory | 1,349,129 | 211,945 | 0.16 | 54% |

▶ **Consolidating your thinking** ◀

Using the outline map of Australia from the Teacher Book (p.50) and the population density data for each state and territory of Australia in the table, construct a choropleth map to show how Australia's population density varies. On a choropleth map, defined areas are shaded according to a graded colour or shading key (as in the example map of global population density shown in Figure A).

Population per sq km
- over 250
- 101 – 250
- 51 – 100
- 11 – 50
- 0 – 10

Figure A

## 5.1 Which environmental factors influence Australia's population distribution?

As the previous activity showed, Australia has one of the world's least dense national populations. In addition to this, the country faces another major geographical challenge because its population is one of the most **spatially** concentrated as the **population distribution** map below shows.

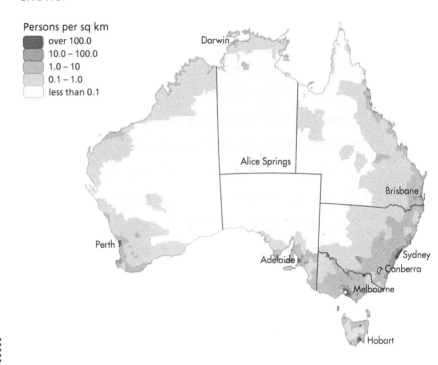

Persons per sq km
- over 100.0
- 10.0 – 100.0
- 1.0 – 10
- 0.1 – 1.0
- less than 0.1

## ▶ Consolidating your thinking ◀

- How does this choropleth map provide a more accurate representation of population distribution compared with the map you constructed in the last exercise?

- Describe the general pattern of population distribution shown on this map and then look at the map of Australia on the previous page to identify specific locations of sparse and dense population using place and state names and locational terms such as 'northeast of', 'along the coast of', etc.

- Close to 600,000 Australians are descended from the indigenous inhabitants of the Australian **continent** and nearby islands. How does the map of the indigenous population centres in the Teacher Book (p.51) compare with the general distribution of the entire population? What are the similarities and differences? Can you suggest reasons for your observations?

All of the maps on this page and the previous page provide information about the physical geography of Australia. Make notes about how each data set helps to explain the distribution of Australia's population. Bear in mind that the **colonisation** and **settlement** of Australia by Europeans was at its height during the period between the 1780s and 1880s.

What would the priorities of these first migrants have been in terms of finding a place to live? Like people moving to a new area today, they would have wanted to maximise benefits and minimise constraints. Share your thinking with a partner and also be prepared to contribute to a general whole group discussion.

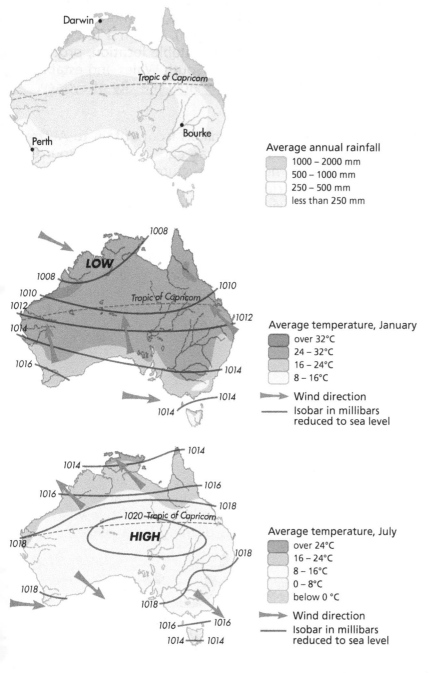

Average annual rainfall
- 1000 – 2000 mm
- 500 – 1000 mm
- 250 – 500 mm
- less than 250 mm

Average temperature, January
- over 32°C
- 24 – 32°C
- 16 – 24°C
- 8 – 16°C

→ Wind direction
— Isobar in millibars reduced to sea level

Average temperature, July
- over 24°C
- 16 – 24°C
- 8 – 16°C
- 0 – 8°C
- below 0 °C

→ Wind direction
— Isobar in millibars reduced to sea level

The satellite image to the right is a simulated natural colour image of Australia, New Zealand and the nearby parts of southeast Asia and the southwest Pacific Ocean. The desert of central and western Australia is shown in pink-brown, whilst the greens on the image show those areas with forests and farmland. Areas of grassland are shown in grey-green.

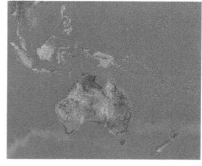

Under the instructions of King George III, the colonisation and settlement of Australia by Britain began in 1788 when Captain Arthur Phillip arrived at Botany Bay with a fleet of eleven ships and about 1000 settlers, of whom 778 were convicts (568 women and 192 men). Within a few days Phillip moved to a much more suitable location, proclaiming the new British colony of New South Wales and establishing the settlement of Sydney Cove, now the city of Sydney.

Sending or 'transporting' criminals from Britain to Australia was carefully planned as a cheap and sustainable source of labour to build the new infrastructure for the colony, creating roads and clearing the land for farming, for example. Many convicts were skilled tradesmen such as stonemasons or farmers who had been convicted of fairly minor and sometimes trivial crimes. Most were sentenced to seven or fourteen years of penal servitude. It was normal for convicts to be issued pardons prior to or on completion of their sentences. When this occurred they were also issued with parcels of land on which to support themselves in the future. Between 1788 and 1868, around 160,000 convicts were sent to Australia from Britain.

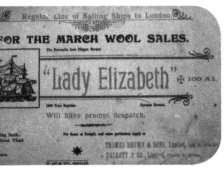

The first 'free settlers' or **immigrants** began to arrive in 1793 and by 1900 the population of Australia had grown from approximately 350,000 indigenous Aborigines in 1788 to a combined population of over four million by 1900. Free settlers were given free passage, a range of agricultural tools, two years' provisions and grants of land on which to farm. They were also allocated convicts to act as free labourers, who came with an allowance of two years' worth of rations as well as enough clothing for a year.

*Early settler map of Sydney Cove*

THE LANDING of the CONVICTS at BOTANY BAY

*'I went out some days ago, about four miles off, to hunt kangaroos; we huntsmen saw five, but the dogs never got sight of them. I went astray returning, and no wonder, for nothing is more perplexing than walking in the bush; you have no object to steer by, except your shadow or a compass; the one is always changing with the day, and the other may mislead, unless you keep your eye constantly upon it.*

*'The country is most singular, but does not possess those features of extreme interest which I expected; there is (as far as I have seen) great sameness in the scenery, and several parties which have been beyond the mountains (perhaps to the distance of 100 miles) report the scenery to be of the same character – undulating ground and extensive plains; but no very striking object, no large rivers, no lakes of any extent – and the low lands are subject to floods in winter. The river on which I have my grant from Government has been but lately discovered, and is not, I believe, navigable; it runs strongly in winter, and forms a series of pools and shallows in summer.'*

From the Journal of George Fletcher Moore, 1834–1841

## ▶ Consolidating your thinking ◀

In terms of building settlements and establishing farms, why would the early settlers of Australia have wanted to stay close to the coast? Reflect on the images and quotation on these two pages and consider how the following would have affected their decision-making:

- As a new colony, Australia would have relied very heavily on **imports** from Britain for its survival.

- The importance of the **export** trade of commodities such as wood and wool to Britain and other countries of Europe.

- How the settlers would have felt about the **marginal** interior of Australia which was so difficult to access.

A mental map is an imagined map of a place and is very useful to geographers because it tells us about the **impression** people have of that place in their mind, rather than what that place may be like in reality. Every individual has a mental map of their surroundings which they carry around in their head and this map is based on their feelings – how safe they feel and how optimistic they are about what the future holds for them, for example.

Thomas Rose, a farmer from Dorset, was amongst the first 'free settlers' to arrive in Australia with his wife and four children in 1793 and was allocated eighty hectares of land for a farm.

Discuss with a partner the mental map of Australia that Thomas would most likely have built up in his mind over the first few years of living in the country. How would this map have been affected by his hopes and fears and the contact he had with other people and the outside world?

Now, on an A3 sheet of paper draw *Thomas Rose's Mental Map of Australia, 1798.* How does your map compare with other people's in the group? What are the main similarities and differences with others?

▶▶

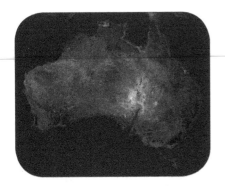

The vast and remote **arid** and **semi-arid** areas of the interior of Australia are often referred to as the 'outback'. Together these areas cover nearly two-thirds of the landmass of the continent. The only continent drier than Australia is Antarctica.

**Tropical – wet summers**
Summers hot to very hot, wet to very wet
Winters mild to warm, dry

**Subtropical – wet summers**
Summers hot, wet, humid
Winters mild, low rainfall

**Temperate – uniform rainfall**
Summers warm to hot, moderate rain
Winters cool to mild, moderate rain

**Temperate – wet winters**
Summers warm to hot, dry
Winters cool to mild, wet

**Subtropical – arid**
Summers hot to very hot, very dry
Winters mild to warm, dry

**Subtropical / Warm Temperate – arid**
Summers hot to very hot, very dry
Winters cool to mild, dry

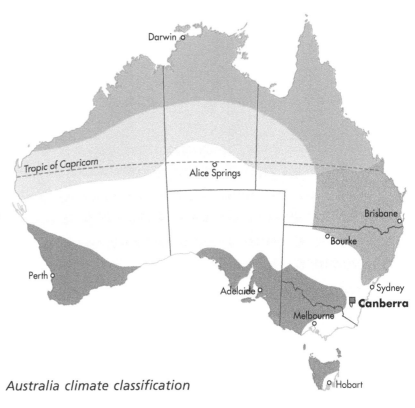

*Australia climate classification*

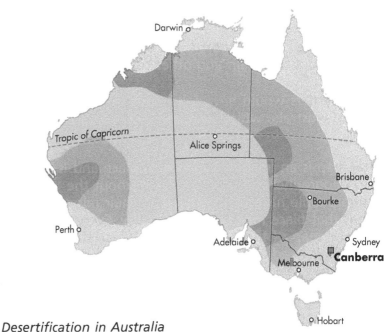

Very high risk of desertification
High risk of desertification
Desert lands

*Desertification in Australia*

## ► Consolidating your thinking ◄

Form a group of five and each choose one of the five places below. Now, draw a climate graph using the model in the Teacher Book (p.52) as a guide, so that all five locations are covered. Once they are finished, the next step is to use the data capture sheet in the Teacher Book (p.53) to compare the characteristics of the climate of the five settlements.

Finally, consider the climatic conditions of each place from the perspective of a cattle or sheep rancher attempting to run a **commercial** farm that will provide a living. Place the five locations in rank order of the opportunities they offer a farmer. Which is the most attractive location and which is the least appealing? How does your rank order compare with those of the other members of your group? Take time to discuss the factors that influenced your decision-making.

Geographers compile climate graphs showing the average weather conditions experienced by a place over at least a thirty-year period for different locations as a way of comparing both the opportunities and constraints the climate creates for people who live there. Below are sets of climate data for five places in Australia which can all be found on the map of climate regions on the previous page.

- Which climatic regions correlate with the arid and semi-arid areas of Australia?
- Which state has the largest proportion of land area classified as desert?
- Which states have no desert?
- Which climate region has the greatest and least concentration of population?

| Alice Springs | Jan | Feb | Mar | Apr | May | Jun | Jul | Aug | Sep | Oct | Nov | Dec |
|---|---|---|---|---|---|---|---|---|---|---|---|---|
| Temperature – max. (°C) | 36 | 35 | 33 | 28 | 23 | 20 | 20 | 23 | 27 | 31 | 34 | 35 |
| Temperature – min. (°C) | 22 | 21 | 18 | 13 | 8 | 5 | 4 | 6 | 10 | 15 | 18 | 20 |
| Rainfall (mm) | 39 | 44 | 32 | 17 | 19 | 14 | 16 | 9 | 8 | 21 | 29 | 37 |

| Sydney | Jan | Feb | Mar | Apr | May | Jun | Jul | Aug | Sep | Oct | Nov | Dec |
|---|---|---|---|---|---|---|---|---|---|---|---|---|
| Temperature – max. (°C) | 26 | 26 | 25 | 22 | 20 | 17 | 16 | 18 | 20 | 22 | 24 | 25 |
| Temperature – min. (°C) | 19 | 19 | 18 | 15 | 12 | 9 | 8 | 9 | 11 | 14 | 16 | 18 |
| Rainfall (mm) | 10 | 118 | 130 | 127 | 120 | 132 | 97 | 81 | 68 | 77 | 84 | 77 |

| Darwin | Jan | Feb | Mar | Apr | May | Jun | Jul | Aug | Sep | Oct | Nov | Dec |
|---|---|---|---|---|---|---|---|---|---|---|---|---|
| Temperature – max. (°C) | 32 | 32 | 33 | 33 | 33 | 31 | 31 | 32 | 33 | 34 | 34 | 33 |
| Temperature – min. (°C) | 25 | 25 | 25 | 24 | 23 | 21 | 19 | 21 | 23 | 25 | 26 | 26 |
| Rainfall (mm) | 386 | 312 | 254 | 97 | 15 | 3 | 0 | 3 | 13 | 51 | 119 | 239 |

| Bourke | Jan | Feb | Mar | Apr | May | Jun | Jul | Aug | Sep | Oct | Nov | Dec |
|---|---|---|---|---|---|---|---|---|---|---|---|---|
| Temperature – max. (°C) | 37 | 36 | 33 | 28 | 23 | 18 | 18 | 21 | 25 | 29 | 34 | 36 |
| Temperature – min. (°C) | 21 | 21 | 18 | 13 | 8 | 6 | 4 | 6 | 9 | 13 | 17 | 19 |
| Rainfall (mm) | 36 | 38 | 28 | 28 | 25 | 28 | 23 | 20 | 20 | 23 | 31 | 36 |

| Perth | Jan | Feb | Mar | Apr | May | Jun | Jul | Aug | Sep | Oct | Nov | Dec |
|---|---|---|---|---|---|---|---|---|---|---|---|---|
| Temperature – max. (°C) | 29 | 29 | 27 | 24 | 21 | 18 | 17 | 18 | 19 | 21 | 24 | 27 |
| Temperature – min. (°C) | 17 | 17 | 16 | 14 | 12 | 10 | 9 | 9 | 10 | 12 | 14 | 16 |
| Rainfall (mm) | 8 | 10 | 20 | 43 | 130 | 180 | 170 | 145 | 86 | 56 | 20 | 13 |

Have a look at the following images. They were all produced during the period 1850–1900.

### ▶ Consolidating your thinking ◀

Examine the images with a partner and discuss what you think they are showing. What are the people doing? What is the surrounding environment like? What clues are there that these images are in the Australian outback?

Listen to the account of Jack Flett at:

http://www.acmi.net.au/vid_poseidon_rush.htm

and read the poem by Henry Lawson on this page. How do Jack's reminiscences and Henry's poem help you to understand the images better?

*The night too quickly passes*
*And we are growing old,*
*So let us fill our glasses*
*And toast the Days of Gold;*
*When finds of wondrous treasure*
*Set all the South ablaze,*
*And you and I were faithful mates*
*All through the roaring days.*

Henry Lawson, *The Roaring Days*, 1889

In 1851, Edward Hargraves discovered a grain of gold in a waterhole in New South Wales. He named the place Ophir. Within four months, 1000 prospectors had moved in and by the end of 1852, 26.4 tonnes of gold had been discovered. During the following year, 370,000 immigrants arrived in Australia as a 'gold rush' gripped the imagination of people from all over the world. By 1871, the population of Australia tripled from 430,000 to 1.7 million. The majority of these migrants were from Britain and other European countries but the second largest foreign contingent (40,000) were Chinese.

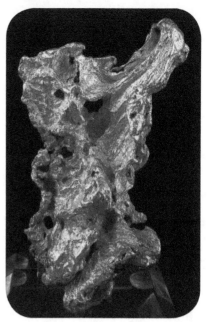

*The largest single gold nugget discovered during the 1850s Australian Gold Rush, measuring 7.4 x 4.4 x 2.3 cm*

## ▷ Consolidating your thinking ◁

Using the base outline map of Australia from the Teacher Book (p.50) and the interactive map at http://www.sbs.com.au/gold/GOLD_MAP.html locate and label each of the thirty-five main places across Australia which formed the focus of the Gold Rush during the years 1850 to 1900. How does the location of these places compare with the places in which most Australians live today?

Today, with 300 million tonnes a year, Australia is the third-largest gold producing country in the world (after China and the US). The mineral makes up 6.5% of the value of the country's exports. Fimiston Open Pit (also known as the Super Pit) in Western Australia is Australia's largest and most productive **open cast** or strip gold mine. It is 3.5 km long, 1.5 km wide and 570 m deep and, with the aid of 550 employees on site, produces thirty tonnes of gold a year.

Open cast or strip mining is a highly controversial method of extracting minerals and fossil fuels from beneath the ground wherever it is proposed in the world. Geographers identify costs and benefits when decisions like how to exploit **natural resources** of any kind have to be made. Using a copy of the table titled '*Advantages and disadvantages of open cast (strip) mining*' in the Teacher Book (p.54) and the additional information provided here produce a summary of the costs and benefits most commonly associated with open cast or strip mining.

### Web links to help with your research:

http://www.ehow.co.uk/info_8280665_open-pit-mining-pros-cons.html

http://www.enviropaedia.com/topic/default.php?topic_id=223

http://digital.library.okstate.edu/encyclopedia/entries/S/SU012.html

http://www.families.com/blog/what-is-surface-mining-and-is-it-bad

https://answers.yahoo.com/question/index?qid=2009
1109171722AApjU7K

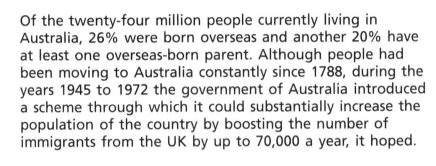

THE STARS WHICH SHINE OVER AUSTRALIA THE LAND OF OPPORTUNITY

THE "SOUTHERN CROSS"

THE CALL OF THE STARS TO BRITISH MEN & WOMEN

★ MEN FOR THE LAND
★ WOMEN FOR THE HOME
★ EMPLOYMENT GUARANTEED
★ GOOD WAGES
★ PLENTY OF OPPORTUNITY

FOR FURTHER INFORMATION APPLY TO ANY EMPLOYMENT EXCHANGE OR TO THE DIRECTOR OF MIGRATION AND SETTLEMENT AUSTRALIA HOUSE, STRAND, W.C.2

**Australian propaganda films:**

Bring out a Briton campaign: https://www.youtube.com/watch?v=dG6zWTLHSrl

Life in Australia – Sydney: https://www.youtube.com/watch?v=vR1CU8NjGW0

Post-war migrants to Australia: https://www.youtube.com/watch?v=0R5OFLabJJA

Ten pound poms commercial: https://www.youtube.com/watch?v=JoY29Y6Y_IQ

Of the twenty-four million people currently living in Australia, 26% were born overseas and another 20% have at least one overseas-born parent. Although people had been moving to Australia constantly since 1788, during the years 1945 to 1972 the government of Australia introduced a scheme through which it could substantially increase the population of the country by boosting the number of immigrants from the UK by up to 70,000 a year, it hoped.

Adults in the UK who were white and under the age of 49 years, along with their family if they had one, could take advantage of an *assisted passage scheme* to Australia. These were the people that the Australian government felt would assimilate most easily into Australian society. Adults paid just £10 (US$16) for a berth on a passenger ship to Australia. Children travelled free. The Australian government also promised the adults work and the family housing and free education. In return, the immigrants had to stay in Australia for at least two years or refund the cost of the journey out (US$120 per person) as well as paying the full cost of their journey home.

Between 1945 and 1972, over one million immigrants from the UK arrived in Australia as 'ten pound poms'. In addition there were also a further 500,000 newcomers at least from other European countries during this time.

### ▶ Consolidating your thinking ◀

In order to attract British immigrants, the Australian government produced propaganda films, television and cinema advertisements and posters which attempted to sell the dream of a modern British life in the sun 'down under'. Watch the films listed in the box to the side and study the poster above. Describe the life that this marketing campaign was trying to sell to British people, who at the time were still suffering food rationing and a serious shortage of housing after the second world war.

Although some immigrants did commit to attempting farming or working on inland construction projects such as the *Snowy Mountains Scheme* (http://en.wikipedia.org/wiki/Snowy_Mountains_Scheme) in the outback, at least 80% of all migrants congregated in the state capital cities. It was in these cities that the majority of the work was available to them and where housing was being built for the new arrivals.

*Ten pound poms on their way to Australia*

## ▶ Consolidating your thinking ◀

With 89% of its people living in cities, Australia is one of the most urbanised countries in the world. In fact, over fifteen million residents of the country (62%) live in the eight state capital cities.

On a copy of the outline map of Australia from the Teacher Book (p.50), draw a located proportional bar of the proportion of the population of each state which lives in its capital city.

| State | Total population | Capital city | Population in capital city |
|---|---|---|---|
| New South Wales | 7,460,000 | Sydney | 4,670,000 |
| Victoria | 5,790,000 | Melbourne | 4,250,000 |
| Queensland | 4,690,000 | Brisbane | 2,190,000 |
| Western Australia | 2,600,000 | Perth | 1,900,000 |
| Southern Australia | 1,680,000 | Adelaide | 1,280,000 |
| Tasmania | 510,000 | Hobart | 220,000 |
| Canberra Capital Territory | 380,000 | Canberra | 380,000 |
| Northern Territory | 240,000 | Darwin | 130,000 |

What does your completed map tell you about the location of the capital cities? If the majority of the 'ten pound poms' moved into these cities, what effect do you think this had on the population distribution of Australia? Did their arrival add to or reduce the domination of coastal areas in Australia?

The state government of New South Wales is trying hard to develop its far west outback with a plan which involves the **economic development** of this interior region. Working in small groups of three or four, try to work out what you think regional development might involve in the outback. If you wanted to encourage people currently living there not to move away to the coast and also persuade immigrants to come there, what sort of things would you need to do to make it attractive? What do the words and phrases in the banner at http://www.rdafarwestnsw.org.au/ such as 'prosperous', 'innovative', 'inclusive', 'economically diverse' and 'sustainable' mean? What kind of place will young adults want to live in?

Since 1995, the government of Australia has been encouraging as many skilled and well qualified immigrants as possible (it allows in approximately 185,000 a year from around the world) to settle in inland rural areas rather than in the major cities along the coast. To achieve this it offers immigrants a very attractive **incentive** package including the following guarantees:

- A local employer with a job offer who will also personally support their application for a visa to work permanently in Australia.

- The right to live and work (along with all their family members if appropriate) permanently.

- The right to study (for themselves and their children) at Australian schools and universities.

- The promise that their application for permanent residency (to include all family members) will be 'fast tracked' – receive priority over the thousands of other applications.

## ► Consolidating your thinking ◄

Since 2011, India has been the source of most of the permanent immigrants each year to Australia and there are now 391,000 people of Indian descent living in the country (2% of the population).

- Describe the distribution of people from India shown in the map of Australia – remember to include the general pattern and also specific places of dense and sparse population you can identify.

- The state of New South Wales is a very popular destination for immigrants from India and there are already 95,000 people of Indian origin living in Sydney and other coastal towns such as Newcastle. *The Times of India* (http://www.timesofindia.indiatimes.com/) is the most widely read English newspaper in India. The state government of New South Wales is intending to place a full page advertisement in this newspaper which they hope will attract migrants from India to inland places such as Bourke, Mildura and Broken Hill rather than Sydney. They have commissioned you to design the advertisement for them. Remember to include the key incentives as well other attractions of the area. You will need to do some background research on the west and northwest areas of New South Wales, e.g. its environment, history, culture and economy, as well as the key towns of Bourke, Mildura and Broken Hill.

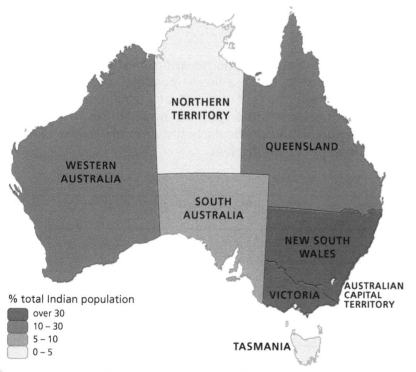

% total Indian population

- over 30
- 10 – 30
- 5 – 10
- 0 – 5

*Population of Indian descent in Australia*

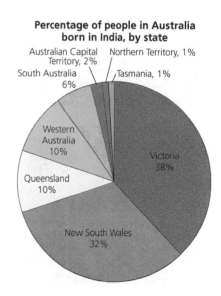

**Percentage of people in Australia born in India, by state**

- Australian Capital Territory, 2%
- Northern Territory, 1%
- South Australia 6%
- Tasmania, 1%
- Western Australia 10%
- Queensland 10%
- Victoria 38%
- New South Wales 32%

## 5.7 How can the Pilbara region of Western Australia be developed sustainably?

The Pilbara covers a remote area of 507,896 km² in Western Australia (over twice the size of the UK), stretching all the way from the Indian Ocean to the border with the Northern Territory. Only 66,298 people live in the entire area of the Pilbara, compared with the 63.7 million residents of the UK.

**The Pilbara Region, Western Australia**

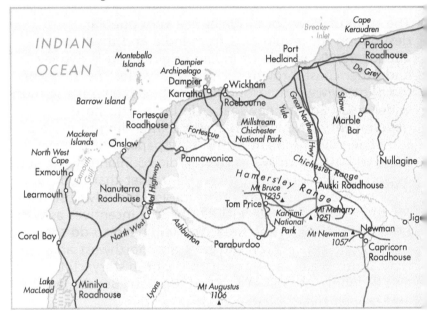

500 – 1000 m
200 – 500 m
0 – 200 m

—— Road
—— Railway

▶ **Consolidating your thinking** ◀

Using evidence from the images and climate data on this page and the next, make a list of possible constraints (things which will make it difficult or a challenge) that are likely to influence whether people move to live in the Pilbara region. Think particularly how people might earn a living and support themselves.

| Port Hedland | Jan | Feb | Mar | Apr | May | Jun | Jul | Aug | Sep | Oct | Nov | Dec |
|---|---|---|---|---|---|---|---|---|---|---|---|---|
| Temperature – max. (°C) | 36 | 36 | 37 | 35 | 31 | 28 | 27 | 29 | 32 | 35 | 36 | 37 |
| Temperature – min. (°C) | 26 | 26 | 25 | 21 | 17 | 14 | 12 | 13 | 15 | 18 | 21 | 24 |
| Rainfall (mm) | 64 | 94 | 49 | 22 | 27 | 24 | 11 | 5 | 1 | 1 | 3 | 20 |

| Newman | Jan | Feb | Mar | Apr | May | Jun | Jul | Aug | Sep | Oct | Nov | Dec |
|---|---|---|---|---|---|---|---|---|---|---|---|---|
| Temperature – max. (°C) | 39 | 37 | 36 | 32 | 26 | 22 | 22 | 25 | 29 | 34 | 37 | 38 |
| Temperature – min. (°C) | 25 | 24 | 22 | 18 | 13 | 10 | 8 | 10 | 14 | 18 | 21 | 24 |
| Rainfall (mm) | 51 | 80 | 39 | 25 | 23 | 25 | 13 | 11 | 4 | 4 | 10 | 27 |

There are currently 45,000 people working in the Pilbara and 18,500 of these jobs are in iron ore mining industries alone. Iron ore is Australia's largest export commodity and of the 400 million tonnes which it sells abroad each year to countries such as China and Japan, 95% comes from the Pilbara. Exports of Pilbara iron ore earn the Australian government US$46 billion a year.

In addition to this, the Pilbara produces 85% and 70% respectively of Australia's **crude oil** and **natural gas**, extracted from the off shore Carnarvon Basin. Other important minerals mined here include salt, silver, gold and manganese.

## ▶ Consolidating your thinking ◀

Look at the two sets of data below and a copy of the Pilbara Regional Community Profile in the Teacher Book (p.55). The government of Western Australia is worried about what it describes as the Pilbara's lack of **economic diversity**. What do you think this means? What do you think would happen to the people of the Pilbara if either the demand for natural resources from countries overseas or the price of iron ore and other minerals suddenly dropped on international markets? What would this mean for communities in the Pilbara?

| Industry | Jobs |
| --- | --- |
| Mining | 18,500 |
| Construction | 8404 |
| Accommodation & Food Services | 2467 |
| Transport, Postal & Warehousing | 2354 |
| Education & Training | 1527 |
| Manufacturing | 1445 |
| Health Care & Social Assistance | 1424 |
| Administrative & Support Services | 1380 |
| Public Administration & Safety | 1369 |
| Professional, Scientific & Technical Services | 1366 |
| Retail Trade | 1349 |
| Other Services | 1101 |
| Rental, Hiring & Real Estate Services | 689 |
| Wholesale Trade | 626 |
| Electricity, Gas, Water & Waste Services | 456 |
| Agriculture, Forestry & Fishing | 163 |
| Financial & Insurance Services | 144 |
| Arts & Recreation Services | 99 |
| Information Media & Telecommunications | 93 |

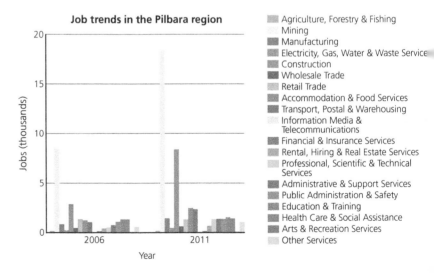

**Job trends in the Pilbara region**

In 1992, the government of Western Australia set up the Pilbara Development Commission to lead and support the sustainable development of the Pilbara. One of its most important aims is to *diversify* the economy of the Pilbara away from being over dependent on the mining industry for most of its wealth and jobs. It also wants to see the number of people living and working in the towns of the Pilbara, such as Newman, to rise to 140,000 by 2035. The Development Commission recognises that if people are to move to the Pilbara then the area must be made as attractive as possible to persuade them to leave the coastal regions of Australia.

Extending your enquiry >>

You have been commissioned by the Pilbara Development Commission (PDC) to advise them on the best way of attracting workers with the right skills to the area by diversifying the **economy** (the kind of jobs that should be created for people outside of mining and construction) and developing the **infrastructure** of the region (the services and facilities people will want, such as housing, schools, shops, leisure amenities, Broadband wireless internet, hospitals and transport links such as road, air and train links). Above all, the PDC wants to see the Pilbara transformed into a more economically balanced and sustainable community for the future.

- Work with a partner and consider what amenities and services you would want to see in a town if you were deciding whether to apply for a job there. Try to identify a top ten priority list.

- How do you think this list of priorities would be different for other people such as a single parent with a three-year-old child or someone looking to set up an internet-based business that will have international clients?

- After successfully obtaining a job what would the top priority need to be for anyone of any age or background moving to the Pilbara?

## Applying your skills

Your recommendations to the PDC will take the form of a ten-minute presentation to the Chief Executive and the Board of Directors. This is not long, therefore you must be careful to ensure that you get key messages and advice across clearly before you run out of time. The Chief Executive is a stickler for time keeping. In your presentation, the PDC particularly wants you to make recommendations about those issues which are described in its Pilbara Regional Development Report which you can find in the Teacher Book (p.56).

**To support your preparation and thinking the following sites will help to get you started:**

http://www.rdapilbara.org.au/

http://www.pdc.wa.gov.au/

http://www.futuredirections.org.au/publications/northern-australia/31-pilbara-prospects-2020-developments-and-challenges-for-the-region.html

http://www.economicprofile.com.au/pilbara

http://rda.gov.au/regions/pilbara

http://www.australiasnorthwest.com/Destinations/The_Pilbara

# 6 Preventing history repeating itself

## What is being done to save Allerford?

Allerford is a small, picturesque village of sixty-seven homes, situated within Exmoor National Park in Somerset, Southwest England. It forms part of the Holnicote Estate owned by the National Trust.

### 6.1 Why is Allerford at risk?

Allerford is at risk. Look at the photographs on this page and the next and the Ordnance Survey map extract on page 90. What clues can you see that might suggest what the risk could be? Discuss what you think with a partner and then contribute your ideas to a group discussion.

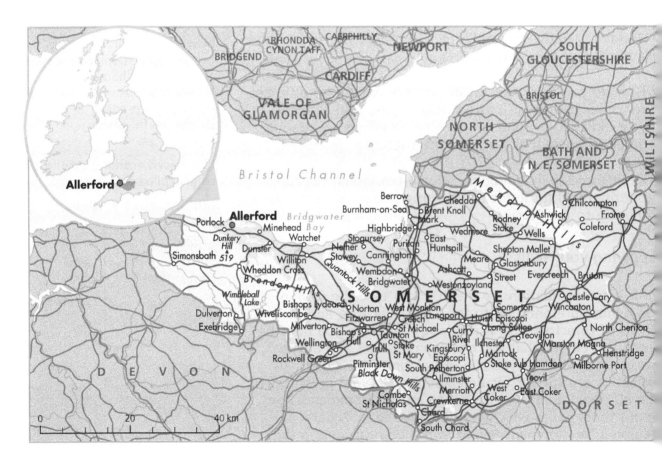

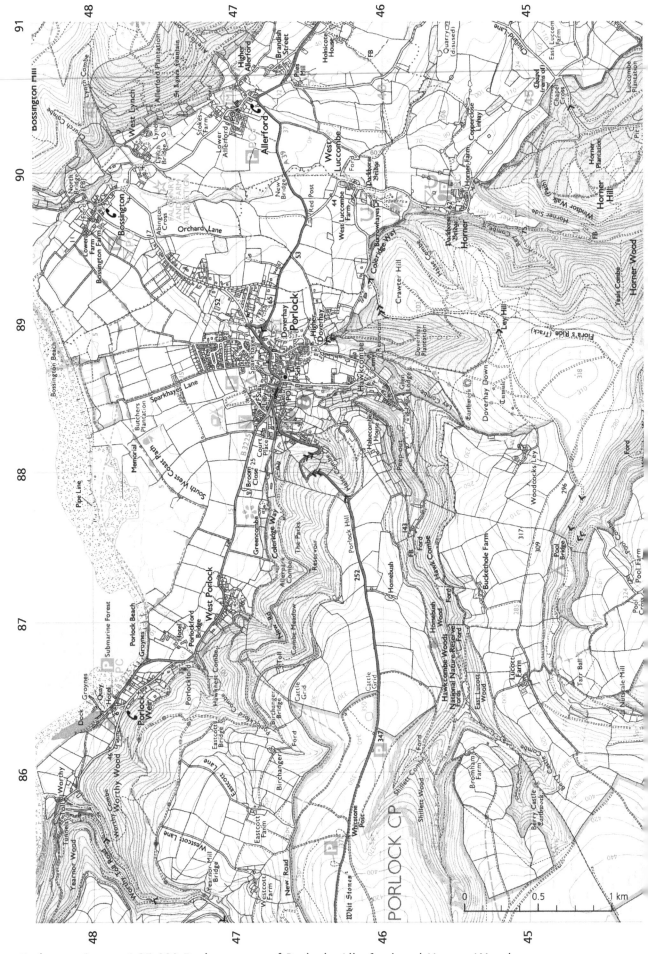

Ordnance Survey 1:25 000 Explorer map of Porlock, Allerford and Horner Wood

## ▶ Consolidating your thinking ◀

The pairs of photographs on this page and the next tell you more about the risk that the village of Allerford faces. The main risk is rapid surface water run off (**flash flooding**) from the **catchment areas** of the River Aller and Horner Water when heavy rainfall occurs in a short period of time. Both catchments are short and steep, falling from 440 m to sea level over just 15 km, resulting in very rapid response times to rainfall events so that river levels rise and fall quickly over a very short time span. The villages downstream from these two rivers are classified by the Environment Agency as **high flood risk**. As well as housing over 200 people, the ninety-eight properties that lie within the flood zone have a combined insurance value of nearly US$50 million.

Have a look at the four pairs of images on this page and the following one. The images show Allerford before and after heavy rain. As you can see, there has been a flash flood.

A.1

A.2

Using the grid in the Teacher Book (p.60), draw a cross section of the **relief** between the top of Ley Hill (spot height 318 m) at 887446 and the view point (spot height 308 m) at 914481.

Annotate your cross section with the following labels:

- Ley Hill
- Halse Combe
- West Lucombe Farm
- Horner Water
- A39
- Allerford village
- River Aller
- Allerford Plantation
- Viewpoint and car park

In what way does your completed cross section help you to understand why the location of the village of Allerford makes it vulnerable to flash flooding after heavy rain?

Allerford is at risk of flash flooding because it is surrounded by **rapid run off river catchments**. Specific characteristics are:

- The very steep hills to the northeast and southeast of the village.

- Numerous **tributary** streams and springs flowing down these hills and joining the two main rivers.

- Although the river valley floor is wide the village is in fact located at its lowest point and squeezed between a **spur** of slightly higher land and the very steep slope of Bossington Hill.

- Both the River Aller (7 km) and the Horner Water (11 km) are short and fairly steep with narrow **channels** throughout their course.

**Trend in average annual rainfall for the UK 1961–2010**

| Dates | Rainfall (mm) |
|-------|---------------|
| 1961–1990 | 1100.6 |
| 1971–2000 | 1126.1 |
| 1981–2010 | 1154.0 |

There is growing concern about the increasing risk of serious flash flooding in Allerford. Evidence from the **Meteorological Office** (http://www.metoffice.gov.uk/news/releases/archive/2013/2012-weather-statistics) suggests that not only is the UK getting more rainfall in total each year but that it is tending to fall in shorter, more intensive bursts. This will create the potential for more frequent flash flooding events in rapid run off catchment areas like Allerford.

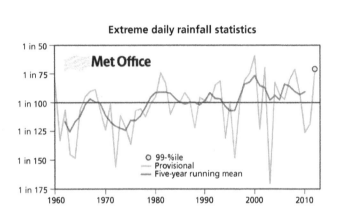

Extreme daily rainfall statistics

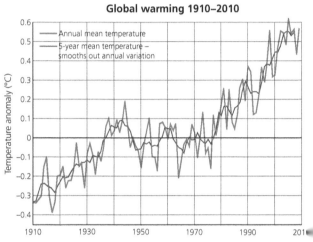

Global warming 1910–2010

The blue line on the rainfall graph above shows how often 1 in every 100 very heavy rainfall days should happen each year in the UK. The red line shows a 'running mean' of what has occurred in reality. What is happening to the number of these 'extreme days' of rainfall over time? Give the figures for a representative number of years to illustrate the trend and to back up your view.

The temperature of the earth's atmosphere has increased by 0.7% during the last 150 years.

Why does this increase the possibility of heavier rain?

Have a look at the article at:

http://www3.imperial.ac.uk/grantham/resources/ipccwg2/ukimpacts/rainfall

## 6.3 What links Allerford to the great Lynmouth flood?

*'As we watched, we saw a row of cottages near the river, in the flashes of lightning because it was dark by this time, fold up like a pack of cards and swept out with the river with the agonising screams of some of the local inhabitants who I knew very well.'*

Ken Oxenholme, a Lynmouth resident, reported by BBC News, 16 August 1952

The disaster, which occurred on the night of 15–16 August 1952 in and around the town of Lynmouth in Devon, just 18 km west along the coast from Allerford, remains the worst river flood experienced in the UK. Over 100 buildings were destroyed and the final death toll reached thirty-four.

PART OF HARBOUR WALL DESTROYED

ROAD AND HOUSES SWEPT AWAY

ORIGINAL COURSE OF WEST LYN R.

NEW COURSE

BRIDGE WRECKED

# ▶ Consolidating your thinking ◀

Recordings of the personal experiences of people who lived through the Lynmouth flood disaster can be found at http://www.exmoor-nationalpark.gov.uk/environment/history/lynmouth-flood-1952/lynmouth-flood-oral-history-resources. News films recorded by the BBC and Pathé News just after the flood at Lynmouth can be viwed at https://www.youtube.com/watch?v=m1xiad4Ppe0 and https://www.youtube.com/watch?v=oLGdKtTFvSw. Listen to these accounts and watch the film footage. Make a note of what they tell you about both the causes and the impact of the flood on the community of Lynmouth.

In the Teacher Book (pp.61-62) there is a page called 'Factors which contributed to causing the Lynmouth flood'. Using a copy of this page:

- Divide the factors into **physical** and **human** causes.

- In the right hand column, write a few notes explaining the effect that you feel each factor might have had in either causing the flood or making its impact worse.

- From the list, try to identify your 'top three' factors which you consider to be the most important when it comes to explaining how serious the flood was. Discuss your choice with those of others in the group. Did everyone make the same choice? Why is it so difficult to pinpoint just one or two factors?

Also in the Teacher Book (p.63) there is a black and white version of the OS map extract of Lynton and Lynmouth which appears on page 99. Stick a copy of this map in the middle of an A3 piece of plain paper and then annotate it with labels to show the location of the causal factors described. Some of your labels will have precise locations, such as 'confluence of East and West Lyn rivers in Lynmouth' whilst others are more general and can be placed where you think is most appropriate, for example 'at the height of the flood, trees as tall as 27 m were uprooted by the rivers as they flowed through wooded areas'.

The photographs on the next page match up with some of the factors mentioned as contributing to the Lynmouth flood. What is the contributing factor from the list in the Teacher Book that links with each of these photographs? Some may link to more than one factor, of course.

Using the outline grid in the Teacher Book (p.64), draw the cross section from 706485 (spot height 316 m) to 748494 (spot height 287 m) and annotate it with the following labels:

- Lydiate Lane

- Lynbridge

- B3234

- West Lyn River

- Oxen Tor Wood

- A39

- East Lyn River

- South Hill Common

Compare your finished cross section with the one you constructed previously for the village of Allerford.

In what ways is the **geomorphology** or shape of the landforms surrounding Lynmouth and Allerford similar?

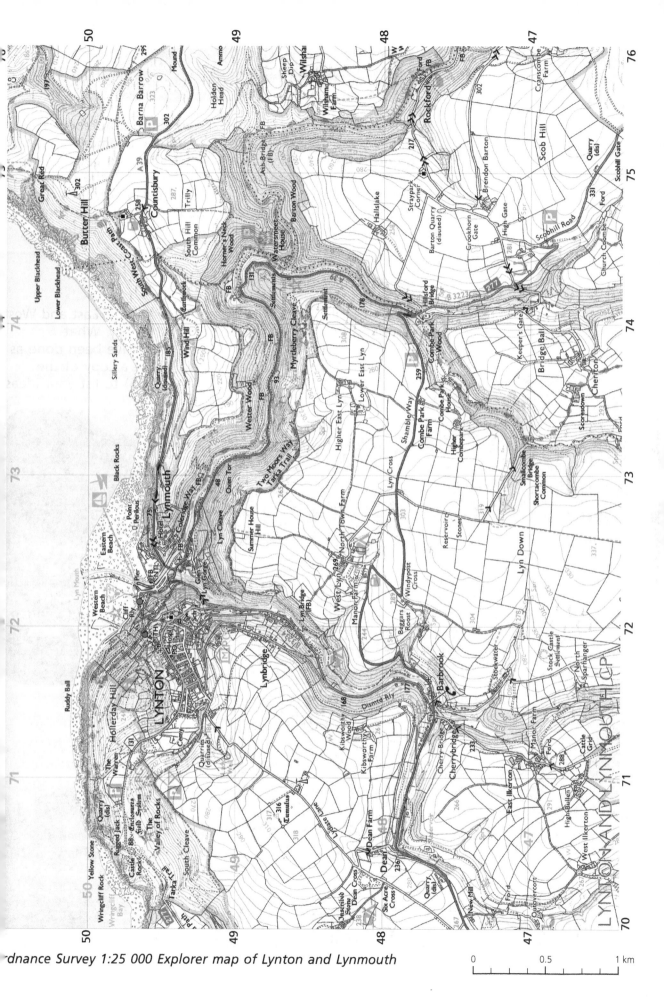

Ordnance Survey 1:25 000 Explorer map of Lynton and Lynmouth

0    0.5    1 km

## 6.4 What has been done at Lynmouth to prevent another flood disaster?

Following the flood disaster at Lynmouth a number of things were done as part of a **flood management programme** to try to prevent a repeat of the devastation. These measures were all aimed at increasing the **capacity** of the entire catchment area of the East and West Lyn rivers to cope with very sudden and heavy rainfall over a short period of time so that flash floods would not occur.

### ▶ Consolidating your thinking ◀

Look carefully at the following images of the East and West Lyn rivers and the village of Lynmouth today. What evidence can you see of the things that have been done as part of the flood management plan? Use a copy of the recording sheet in the Teacher Book (p.65) to list your ideas.

The flood management measures taken at Lynmouth after the flooding included:

- The **mouth** of the East Lyn river was made much wider where it flows out into the sea.

- The course (or route) of the West Lyn river was made much straighter.

- The West Lyn river was allowed to follow its original course to the sea rather than being redirected once again, so:

  o Building restrictions were put in place in Lynmouth, with areas close to the river which are most prone to flooding being left as open spaces such as parks and car parks.

  o Replacement bridges were made wider and taller and often of wood rather than stone.

- Stone and concrete embankments were built alongside the rivers.

- The **confluence** of the East and West Lyn rivers in the centre of Lynmouth was widened and lined with 15 m high walls.

## Consolidating your thinking

Add any of these measures that you have not already identified to your record sheet and write alongside a few notes to explain how you think each might help to reduce the risk of flash flooding at Lynmouth in the future.

Exmoor National Park has just opened a brand new visitor centre in the newly rebuilt Pavilion on the seafront at Lynmouth (http://www.exmoor-nationalpark.gov.uk/visiting/national-park-centres/lynmouth). One of the important things that the centre will do is explain to visitors the causes of the great flash flood in the village.

To help them do this, Ben and Louise, who run the centre, are going to need a number of three-dimensional models of the catchment area of the East and West Lyn rivers so that they can interpret for visitors how the geomorphology of the land surrounding Lynmouth contributed to causing such a deadly flood. Your task is to create a model for the centre using whatever materials you wish. Ideas can be found at http://www.sln.org.uk/geography/just_good_ideas.htm.

Your model needs to show the following features:

- The very steep and deep **gorges** down through which the East and West Lyn rivers flow to the sea.

- The upland areas of Exmoor **moorland** above Lynmouth where the rivers originate.

- The village of Lynmouth.

- The confluence of the East and West Lyn rivers in Lynmouth.

- The mouth of the East and West Lyn rivers in the Bristol Channel.

When designing and constructing your model, use the OS map extract on page 99, together with all of the other resources including the films, photographs and interviews that you have used during your investigation of the Lynmouth floods. Take a photograph of your finished model and email it to Ben or Louise at:

NPCLynmouth@exmoor-nationalpark.gov.uk

More than sixty years on from the Lynmouth flood, the Environment Agency (EA) and the National Trust (NT) are collaborating at Allerford in a three-year programme called the Holnicote Project. This project is funded by the UK government through its Department for Environment, Food and Rural Affairs (DEFRA) with additional funding from the EA and NT. However, its approach to river flood management at Allerford is very different from the action taken after the flood at Lynmouth in the 1960s and 70s.

### ▶ Consolidating your thinking ◀

Take a look at the photographs on this page, the map and aerial photograph of restoration works being undertaken along the River Aller on the next page, and the levee sections design plan in the Teacher Book (p.66). Discuss with a partner how you think creating new sluices on the river and constructing five 1.5 m high shallow-sloping levees (or bunds), ponds and scrapes on the flood plain and water meadows of the River Aller will help to reduce potential flood flows reaching Allerford.

In addition to restoration along the flood plain of the River Aller, the Holnicote Project team is also working high up in the moorland catchments and **headwaters** of the River Aller and Horner Water, which can receive more than 2000 mm of rain a year. Once again the objective here is to slow down run off water from the hills that might result in a flash flood. Old **drainage ditches** and drovers' tracks have been particularly targeted. What has the Holnicote Project team done every 30 m or so to the drains and tracks? How do you think it is helping to regulate the flow of water?

Finally, the project team has also been working in the woodland that covers the steep slopes of the river catchments. Through this woodland hundreds of tributary streams flow very quickly down steep transitional valleys to the rivers Aller and Horner Water below. The policy of removing fallen timber and woody debris from the course of the rivers has been relaxed. What is being done with the fallen wood now? How will this help to achieve the overall objective of controlling run off and preventing sudden flash floods downstream at Allerford?

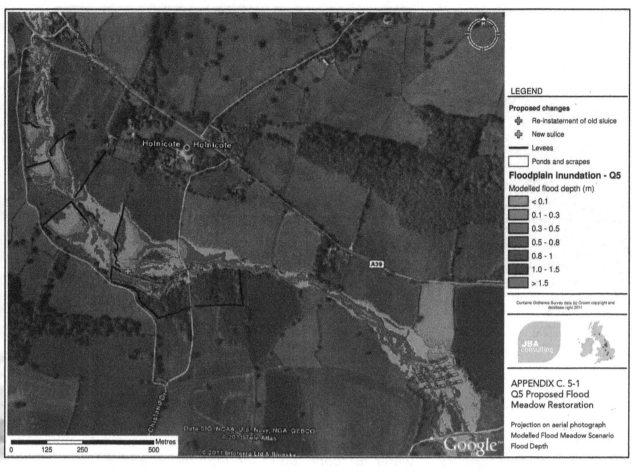

LEGEND

**Proposed changes**

✚ Re-instatement of old sluice

✚ New sluice

━━━ Levees

▭ Ponds and scrapes

**Floodplain inundation - Q5**

Modelled flood depth (m)

░ < 0.1

░ 0.1 - 0.3

░ 0.3 - 0.5

░ 0.5 - 0.8

░ 0.8 - 1

░ 1.0 - 1.5

░ > 1.5

Contains Ordnance Survey data © Crown copyright and database right 2011

JBA Consulting

APPENDIX C. 5-1
Q5 Proposed Flood
Meadow Restoration

Projection on aerial photograph
Modelled Flood Meadow Scenario
Flood Depth

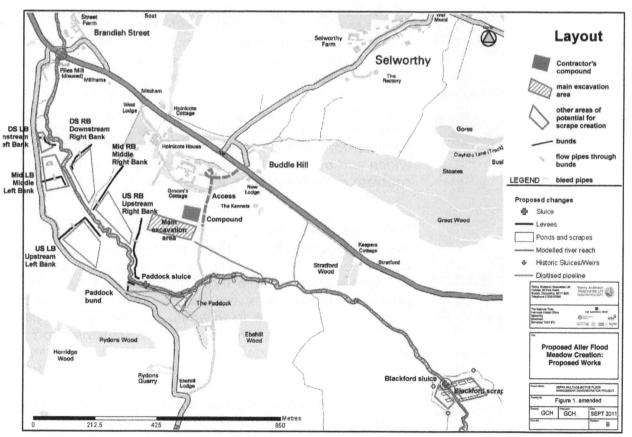

**Layout**

▪ Contractor's compound

▨ main excavation area

◇ other areas of potential for scrape creation

━ bunds

ᐟ flow pipes through bunds

LEGEND ⸺ bleed pipes

**Proposed changes**

✚ Sluice

━━━ Levees

▭ Ponds and scrapes

⸺ Modelled river reach

✤ Historic Sluices/Weirs

⸺ Digitised pipeline

**Proposed Aller Flood
Meadow Creation:
Proposed Works**

Figure 1. amended

| Drawn | Originator | Date |
|-------|-----------|------|
| GCH | GCH | SEPT 2011 |

The winter of 2013/2014 in the UK was the wettest since 1910 and the stormiest for more than twenty years, as twelve serious storms tracked across the country. There was major flooding in many places including the Somerset Levels and large sections of the valley of the River Thames but *not* in Allerford. This was a cause of great relief and delight for Nigel Hester, project manager for the National Trust at the Holnicote Estate Office, as he describes below.

'Our river flood management scheme is all about slowing river water down and regulating its flow to reduce flood risk, rather than trying to hold it back behind massive man made constructions such as dams and reservoirs or building huge concrete embankments and perhaps even changing the course of rivers completely. It's all about working with nature rather than battling against it.

'With the amount of rain we had last winter which went on for over two months, I was amazed that no one in Allerford got flooded. It shows that our scheme to encourage rain water to "pool" up in the high moors and then flow down slowly through streams and rivers with woody debris dams before reaching scrapes, wet woods and bunds in the valley is working to reduce flood risk to villagers. In fact early data analysis indicates that these measures have reduced the flood peak along the River Aller by 12% and no properties have flooded despite an extraordinary wet winter. In the past managing flooding along rivers was all about control and getting rid of the water as quickly as possible downstream which often involved drastic steps to widen and deepen river channels and to construct tall concrete embankments beside the river.

'This is what happened at Lynmouth after the 1952 flood. Areas of housing close to the river which were devastated by the flood were never built on again and taller and stronger bridges replaced those that had been lost. The policy at Lynmouth was very much around using a "hard engineering" approach to solving a problem whereas here at Allerford we have gone for a more sustainable "soft engineering" strategy which some people tell us is "going back to nature". What we are doing here has much less impact on the environment than schemes involving a hard engineering response to situations. In fact our project has actually contributed to broadening biodiversity.

'For example, the new scrapes and ponds on the floodplain that we have created to retain and slowly release flood water back into the river also offer an ideal habitat for wading birds.

'It's important though that people realise that soft engineering can not only deliver great results but also that it can deliver those results cost effectively. The Holnicote project which has been going since 2009 has cost £1 million [US$1.6 million]. That sounds a lot but when you consider that what we have put into place is protecting £30 million [US$49 million] of property that would otherwise be at risk, it's a great deal!'

## Applying your skills

Around 54% of the world's population (over 3.5 billion people) now live in **urban** areas. Managing the risk of flooding in towns and cities, therefore, is just as important as thinking through the most sustainable option in rural places such as Exmoor. Urban areas cover 10% of the UK and nearly fifty million people live in them. When heavy rain falls in short bursts over towns and cities, pluvial flooding occurs as water flows over the surface of concrete and tarmac without draining away. Soft engineering approaches are also being used to manage this risk of urban pluvial flooding.

Read through the online information at the sites below and make a note of four examples of things that are already being done to manage flooding in cities such as Seattle in the United States.

- http://sustainablecities collective.com/david-thorpe/292016/ten-ways-manage-flood-risk-designing-exceedance

- http://www.susdrain.org/delivering-suds/drainage-exceedance/stakeholders/floods-in-urban-areas.html

  http://www.seattle.gov/util/groups/public/@spu/@usm/documents/webcontent/spu02_019984.pdf

Another approach to managing urban flood risk is to design and construct homes that float as can be seen at http://www.inspirationgreen.com/floating-homes.html and http://www.bbc.co.uk/news/technology-20502736.

As a final exercise, design and describe a simple yet practical idea of your own for managing flood water in towns and cities that could be incorporated by architects into individual new properties, streets or housing estates.

Explain how it would be an effective way of reducing the risk of flooding and don't forget to patent it!

# 7 The world's other population problem

What should the European Union do about its declining population?

For most of history, the population of the world has remained fairly constant and fairly low. However, in the last couple of hundred years since the **Industrial Revolution**, the global population has increased exponentially from one billion in 1804 to nearly 7.3 billion today. Much of this population growth is in the less economically developed countries of the world, where births significantly outstrip deaths.

Oman topped the population growth rate table with an average growth rate between 2010 and 2015 (estimated) of just over 8% per year, although growth rates between 2 and 4% were typical for most **Sub-Saharan African countries**. These countries are described as being at stage 2 of the **Demographic Transition Model**, a graph which illustrates how populations change over time with regards to births, deaths and total population growth. Countries at stage 2 and stage 3 (which is characterised by low **death rates** and decreasing **birth rates**) typically have to deal with a range of issues associated with rapid population growth. Some of these are environmental; air, water and soil pollution and shortages of arable land and fresh water supplies can make living conditions difficult. These countries also tend to have a very **youthful population** structure which means that there are large numbers of people dependent upon those that are working and high unemployment rates, which sometimes leads to political unrest. For these countries this is a population problem caused by the rapid increases in the number of people.

| World population (billion) | Year population milestone reached | Years elapsed between milestones |
|---|---|---|
| 1 | 1804 | x |
| 2 | 1925 | 121 |
| 3 | 1959 | 34 |
| 4 | 1974 | 15 |
| 5 | 1987 | 13 |
| 6 | 1999 | 12 |
| 7 | 2012 | 13 |
| 8 | 2026 (est.) | 14 |

However, this enquiry is not about those countries, nor is it about rapid population growth and the problems that it causes in the less economically developed countries of the world. Instead, this enquiry turns its attention to focus upon the causes and responses to population decline in the more economically developed countries of the European Union. It highlights that, instead of having one significant population problem, the world actually has two, which are equally as urgent and problematic.

## World population growth

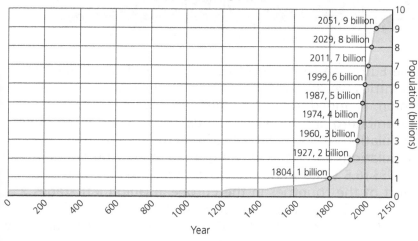

- 2051, 9 billion
- 2029, 8 billion
- 2011, 7 billion
- 1999, 6 billion
- 1987, 5 billion
- 1974, 4 billion
- 1960, 3 billion
- 1927, 2 billion
- 1804, 1 billion

## Demographic Transition Model

| Stage | 1 High stationary | 2 Early expanding | 3 Late expanding | 4 Low stationary | 5? Declining? |
|---|---|---|---|---|---|
| **Examples** | A few remote groups | Egypt, Kenya, India | Brazil | USA, Japan, France, UK | Germany |
| **Birth rate** | High | High | Falling | Low | Very low |
| **Death rate** | High | Falls rapidly | Falls more slowly | Low | Low |
| **Natural increase** | Stable or slow increase | Very rapid increase | Increase slows down | Stable or slow increase | Slow decrease |
| **Reasons for changes in birth rate** | Many children needed for farming. Many children die at an early age. Religious/social encouragement. No family planning. | | Improved medical care and diet. Fewer children needed. | Family planning. Good health. Improving status of women. Later marriages. | |
| **Reasons for changes in death rate** | Disease, famine. Poor medical knowledge so many children die. | Improvements in medical care, water supply and sanitation. Fewer children die. | | Good health care. Reliable food supply. | |

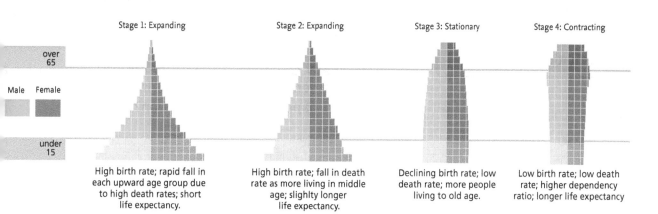

**Stage 1: Expanding** — High birth rate; rapid fall in each upward age group due to high death rates; short life expectancy.

**Stage 2: Expanding** — High birth rate; fall in death rate as more living in middle age; slighlty longer life expectancy.

**Stage 3: Stationary** — Declining birth rate; low death rate; more people living to old age.

**Stage 4: Contracting** — Low birth rate; low death rate; higher dependency ratio; longer life expectancy

Male   Female

over 65

under 15

The European Union (EU) is a collection of twenty-eight countries which work together in political and economic union. Founded in 1952 by Belgium, France, Germany, Luxembourg and the Netherlands, today it has a combined population of 500 million (7.3% of the total global population) and generates a **gross domestic product (GDP)** of US$16.5 trillion, the second highest GDP in the world. Most of the countries in the European Union left stages 2 and 3 of the Demographic Transition Model behind several decades ago and currently sit in stage 4 (low births and low deaths resulting in a stable population) or stage 5 (births fall below deaths resulting in a shrinking population).

### ▶ Consolidating your thinking ◀

- Which countries are members of the European Union and when did they join? Use the map in the Teacher Book (pp.69–70) to shade in the countries according to their accession.

- Which countries are in Europe but not members of the EU? Why do you think they have decided not to join?

- The countries in the EU have varying levels of development. Is this a problem or an opportunity? Why do you think this? Use the data and the questions in the Teacher Book (pp.69–70) to help you.

- Are most populations in the EU increasing or decreasing? Is this mainly due to natural change or migration? What stage of the Demographic Transition Model are the different countries of the EU at? Complete the sheet 'Questioning the data' in the Teacher Book (pp.71–72), which analyses the data shown in the European Union population data table and will help you to answer these questions.

- Are there any countries in the EU which are heading for a 'stage 6' of demographic transition. If so, what do you think could happen to the population?

Read the information sheet 'Designing a new demographic model' in the Teacher Book (p.73). You can use this information to come up with a new, up-to-date and more relevant model.

You might want to keep drafting and altering your model as you move through the enquiry and come across new information.

# European Union population data table

| Country | Birth rate<br>per 1000<br>population per year | Death rate<br>per 1000<br>population per year | Natural change<br>per 1000<br>population per year | Net migration<br>per 1000<br>population per year | Overall growth<br>or decline?<br>per 1000 population<br>per year |
|---|---|---|---|---|---|
| Belgium | 9.99 | 10.76 | -0.77 | 1.22 | 0.45 |
| Bulgaria | 8.92 | 14.30 | -5.38 | -2.89 | -8.27 |
| Czechia<br>(Czech Republic) | 9.79 | 10.29 | -0.50 | 2.15 | 1.65 |
| Denmark | 10.22 | 10.23 | -0.01 | 2.25 | 2.24 |
| Germany | 8.42 | 11.29 | -2.87 | 1.06 | -1.81 |
| Estonia | 10.29 | 13.69 | -3.40 | -3.37 | -6.77 |
| Ireland | 15.18 | 6.45 | 8.73 | 3.31 | 12.04 |
| Greece | 8.80 | 11.00 | -2.20 | 2.32 | 0.12 |
| Spain | 9.88 | 9.00 | 0.88 | 7.24 | 8.12 |
| France | 12.49 | 9.06 | 3.43 | 1.09 | 4.52 |
| Croatia | 9.49 | 12.13 | -2.64 | 1.43 | -1.21 |
| Italy | 8.84 | 10.10 | -1.26 | 4.29 | 3.03 |
| Cyprus | 11.44 | 6.57 | 4.87 | 9.89 | 14.76 |
| Latvia | 9.79 | 13.60 | -3.81 | -2.37 | -6.18 |
| Lithuania | 9.36 | 11.55 | -2.19 | -0.73 | -2.92 |
| Luxembourg | 11.75 | 8.53 | 3.22 | 7.97 | 11.19 |
| Hungary | 9.26 | 12.72 | -3.46 | 1.34 | -2.12 |
| Malta | 10.24 | 8.96 | 1.28 | 1.99 | 3.27 |
| Netherlands | 10.83 | 8.57 | 2.26 | 1.97 | 4.23 |
| Austria | 8.76 | 10.38 | -1.62 | 1.76 | 0.14 |
| Poland | 9.77 | 10.37 | -0.60 | -0.47 | -1.07 |
| Portugal | 9.42 | 10.97 | -1.55 | 2.74 | 1.19 |
| Romania | 9.27 | 11.88 | -2.61 | -0.24 | -2.85 |
| Slovenia | 8.54 | 11.25 | -2.71 | 0.37 | -2.34 |
| Slovakia | 10.01 | 9.70 | 0.31 | 0.01 | 0.32 |
| Finland | 10.35 | 10.51 | -0.16 | 0.62 | 0.46 |
| Sweden | 11.92 | 9.45 | 2.47 | 5.46 | 7.93 |
| United<br>Kingdom | 12.22 | 9.34 | 2.88 | 2.56 | 5.44 |

All figures from 2014 CIA World Factbook

Population naturally declines when the death rate is higher than the birth rate which, in 2014, was the case for nearly two-thirds of EU countries. Therefore, in order to explain the causes of the population decline we need to look at both sides of the equation; what is causing death rates to be so low in the EU and what is causing birth rates to fall so dramatically that they are lower than death rates?

### Low death rates

The main reason for low death rates in the European Union is due to the fact that life expectancy (the average number of years one can expect to live to at birth) has been increasing. In 2012, **life expectancy** for the twenty-eight EU countries was 80.3 years, an increase of 2.6 years in the decade since 2002. Whilst life expectancy is rising for all countries, there are still significant differences between and within countries, and also between males and females (although the gender gap is slowly closing). For example, there is a gap in life expectancy of 11.5 years between the lowest life expectancy for males in the EU, Lithuania (68.4 years), and the highest, Sweden (79.9 years).

The biggest impact on life expectancy has arguably been the reduction in **infant mortality**; between 1997 and 2012 this rate was almost halved. Those countries which still have relatively high rates – Romania with 9.0 per 1000 and Bulgaria with 7.8 per 1000 – have still seen significant decreases, down from 22.0 and 17.5 in 1997 respectively.

The increase in life expectancy can also be attributed to:

• increased living standards

• improved lifestyles

• better education

• better healthcare.

Look at the images which show increased living standards, improved lifestyles, better education and better healthcare. Why do you think that these things result in an increased life expectancy and therefore lower death rates? Try to link your ideas together if you can.
▶▶

## Low birth rates

**Fertility rates** started to decline in the twenty-eight EU countries around the mid-1960s and continued to do so until the turn of the century. However, in the last few years and particularly since 2009, most countries have seen a small increase in the total fertility rate. **Replacement rate** – the number of births per woman needed to keep the population constant – is 2.1. However, the number of births per woman in the EU has been much lower than this in recent years. It was 1.45 births per woman in 2002 and 1.58 births per woman in 2012. This slight increase may be due to women delaying having children until they are older; many women are choosing to have a career before they start a family. In fact, the average age for women to have their first child in the EU in 2012 was 30.1 years, which had increased from 29.1 in 2002.

Read the article at:

http://www.forbes.com/
sites/joelkotkin/2012/05/
30/whats-really-behind-
europes-decline-its-the-
birth-rates-stupid/

which describes how
the Eurozone economic
crisis may be a result
of some countries'
attitude to birth rates.
►►

## Migration

So far, our enquiry has mainly focused on decline of population in the EU as a result of **natural change**. However, another important factor is **net migration** – how people move around and between countries. In fact, many of the countries in the EU that have seen a natural decline in their population have actually seen their total populations rise as a result of positive net migration.

People living within the EU have the right to live and work in, and therefore move freely between, any of the member states. As a consequence, in 2008, more than a quarter of migrants into the UK came from other EU countries and over 48,000 UK citizens moved to Spain, France and Germany. Generally, the wealthier countries in the EU tend to attract migrants from the poorer nations in the group. When the A8 countries – Czechia (Czech Republic), Estonia, Hungary, Latvia, Lithuania, Poland, Slovakia and Slovenia – joined the EU in 2004, one of the largest migrations in history occurred with estimates ranging from 600,000 to 1.4 million Eastern Europeans moving into the UK. The positives and negatives have been well documented, however for most the migration was temporary. After the UK moved into economic recession in 2008, many of the A8 migrants returned to their original countries.

More recently, as restrictions for Bulgarians and Romanians to move freely into the UK have been lifted, some people have been concerned that this will lead to another massive influx of population. However, initial analyses of statistics suggest that, rather than dramatically increasing, the number of migrants from these countries has actually decreased. You can read more about this at http://www.bbc.co.uk/news/uk-politics-21523319.

Population decline doesn't mean that in a few years there will be nobody left within the country, but it does mean that, left unchecked, the population will become an ageing one. In 1950, the **median age** of the population of the EU was 30 years, whereas today it is 40 years. Estimates suggest that by 2050 it will be 47; ten years older than Asia's median age will be and twenty years older than Africa's median age will be. Whilst having a large proportion of older people can be an advantage – those who are retired are more likely to volunteer within their local communities and provide childcare for grandchildren, which saves vast amounts of money for working parents – it can also bring difficulties. For example, it means that there are proportionally fewer people in the workforce, which may result in a loss of innovation and skills and a smaller pension pot for an ever-increasing number of retirees. Also, more elderly people are likely to rely more on specialised healthcare services such as hip replacements (which cost between US$12,000 and US$18,000 per operation) and heart bypasses (costing around US$33,000), which can cause a strain on services such as the National Health Service (NHS) in the UK.

The attitudes to Europe's population problem are varied, with some concerned about potential lack of economic growth, lack of defence and an increased healthcare demand. However, others view population decline positively, suggesting that the reduction in density and congestion may result in a more sustainable environmental situation, particularly with regards to global warming.

### ▶ Consolidating your thinking ◀

What are some of the advantages and disadvantages of a declining population? Write some suggestions in a table. For each disadvantage can you think of a practical solution?

So how can the EU solve its population problem? Deaths are likely to stay fairly static so either the countries have to focus on increasing their fertility rates or on encouraging migration between countries (or both!).

The EU's open migration policy has resulted in significant movement between countries to the extent that twenty-two of the twenty-eight member states have seen positive net migration in recent years. For most this means that even though their populations are naturally declining, they are actually seeing a net increase as migrants cross country boundaries.

Again, there are social and economic advantages and disadvantages for both the origin and destination countries.

You could use the information sheet in the Teacher Book (p.74) to structure your thinking and to help you to consider what the population situation in the UK would be like if it was no longer a member of the EU.

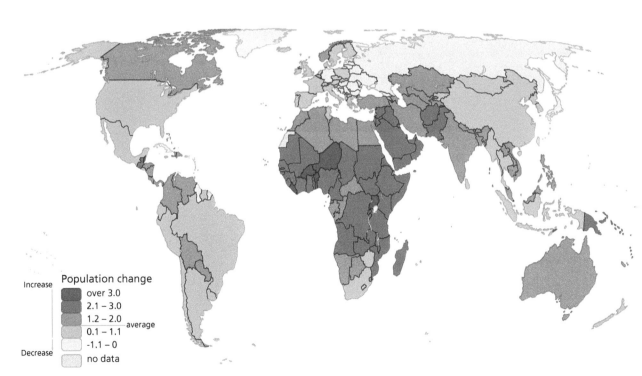

*Map of world population change*

Much harder for governments to control are birth rates, but EU countries are looking to other parts of the world for creative ideas to boost fertility. Singapore has combined an ad campaign with financial incentives – it offers US$12,000 and extended maternity leave – to increase its 0.78 children per woman fertility rate. Its Urban Development Authority has also placed a limit on the building of one bedroom flats in an attempt to encourage people to live together. In South Korea, their low birth rate is largely a result of concerns parents have that they will not be able to afford childcare and education. The government have halved tuition fees to try to allay these concerns, but they have also taken a more creative approach by insisting that offices turn off their lights at 7 p.m. every third Wednesday of the month so that employees can go home for 'Family Day'.

Elsewhere, in Japan, students at the University of Tsukuba have created Yotaro, a robot baby. The robot mimics a real baby by sneezing, giggling and crying and the students hope that it will trigger the emotions of being a parent so that people who own them will want to have their own babies.

In France, the government has created a number of policies to encourage people to have more children. These are known as **pro-natalist policies**. Take a look at Figure A, a diagram which shows some of France's pro-natalist policies.

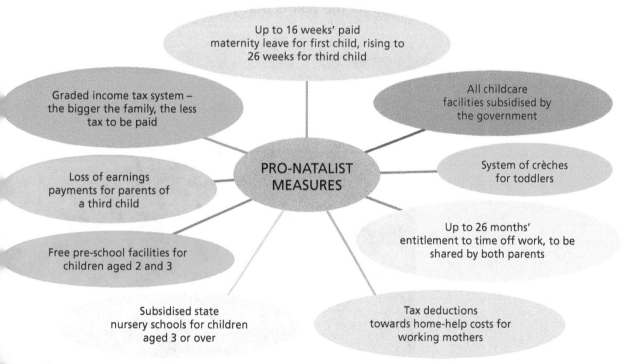

Up to 16 weeks' paid maternity leave for first child, rising to 26 weeks for third child

Graded income tax system – the bigger the family, the less tax to be paid

All childcare facilities subsidised by the government

Loss of earnings payments for parents of a third child

PRO-NATALIST MEASURES

System of crèches for toddlers

Free pre-school facilities for children aged 2 and 3

Up to 26 months' entitlement to time off work, to be shared by both parents

Subsidised state nursery schools for children aged 3 or over

Tax deductions towards home-help costs for working mothers

Figure A

## Sources of further information:

http://yaleglobal.yale.edu/content/fewer-babies-pose-difficult-challenges-europe

http://www.nytimes.com/2013/08/14/world/europe/germany-fights-population-drop.html?pagewanted=all&_r=0

http://www.washingtonpost.com/blogs/worldviews/wp/2013/10/31/how-the-worlds-populations-are-changing-in-one-map/

http://www.pop.org/content/fertility-decline-in-western-europe-1727

http://content.time.com/time/specials/packages/article/0,28804,2097720_2097782_2097841,00.html

## ▷ Consolidating your thinking ◁

You are going to *write a presentation* to bring all of this information together and help you answer the key question at the beginning of the enquiry. You need to use the information covered so far, plus further reading of your own (additional sources are recommended in the side box) to *demonstrate that you understand* that the declining population of the EU is an important problem which has a range of implications and solutions.

- Firstly, you need to decide on your mode of presentation. You could use PowerPoint or Prezi (www.prezi.com), but equally you could use something a little different such as GoAnimate (www.goanimate.com). Whatever format you decide upon, you must remember that you need to engage your audience, so don't put too much text or information up at once.

- You then need to plan your presentation so that it answers the key question: *What should the European Union do about its declining population?* Break this question down into smaller sub-questions (you can use the structure of this enquiry to help you) to set the scene.

- Towards the end of your presentation you should suggest some practical things that the EU could do to solve the problem of their declining population. You may want to focus on the EU as a whole or on a specific country. Include statistics, figures, graphs, maps and images to support the points that you make.

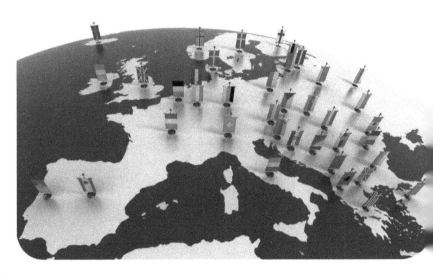

## 7.5 Why is the UK bucking the EU trend?

Despite the general trend of population decline highlighted in the majority of the EU countries, in the last few years the UK has actually experienced an increase in its population, both in terms of its natural change and migration. Fertility rates have actually increased from 1.64 children per woman in 2001 to 1.97 children per woman in 2008 and, as a consequence, its population is growing at a rate of 5.44 people per 1000 per year. Much of this increase has been explained by the fertility rates of migrants, who are more likely to have larger families than British-born mothers. However, it has also been suggested that policies to reduce child poverty may also have had an impact. You can read more about this at http://www.bbc.co.uk/news/uk-13809280.

### ▶ Consolidating your thinking ◀

• Which other EU countries are in a similar position to the UK in experiencing a rise in population? Carry out some research into the populations of one of these countries. Why do you think their population is increasing?

Does this additional information about the UK's demographic situation change your argument as to whether or not the UK should remain in the EU after 2017? Can you explain your answer?

• Use the activity in the Teacher Book (p.75) to complete the population odd one out grid. Look at the four words in each row of the grid. Which is the odd one out? For each, justify your answer. For the last row, can you make up your own odd one out puzzle?

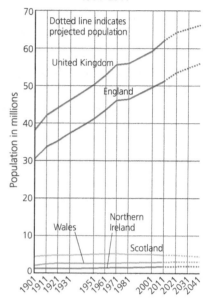

Increase in UK population, 1901–2041

### Sources of information:

http://www.bbc.co.uk/news/health-11960183

http://www.bbc.co.uk/news/uk-18854762

http://www.populationmatters.org/wp-content/uploads/population_problem_uk.pdf

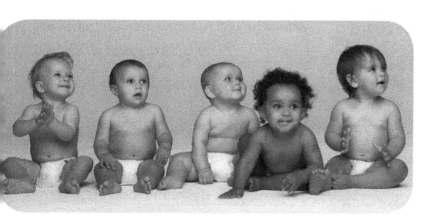

# Glossary

## A

**abrasion** a process of erosion where rocks embedded in the glacier scrape away at the surrounding rock

**aftershock** a smaller earthquake following the main shock of a large earthquake

**albedo** the amount of light or heat radiated by a surface. Light surfaces tend to reflect more heat than dark surfaces, which absorb more

**alluvial soil** a fine-grained fertile soil deposited by water flowing over flood plains or in river beds

**Arctic** the regions around the North Pole, north of the Arctic Circle (66° 33' 44" N)

**arête** a sharp-edged mountain ridge

**arid** having little or no rain; too dry or barren to support vegetation

**aspect** the direction in which a particular thing is facing e.g. north facing aspect

## B

**backwall** the steep, curved rock at the head of a corrie

**bay** a broad inlet of the sea where the land curves inwards

**bedrock** solid rock found under loose deposits such as soil

**birth rate** the number of babies born per 1000 of the population per year

## C

**Canterbury Earthquake Recovery Authority (CERA)** an organisation set up to assist in the recovery and rebuild following the 2010 and 2011 earthquakes in Christchurch, NZ

**catchment area** the area of land from which rainfall flows into a river, lake or reservoir

**central business district (CBD)** the central zone of a town or city, characterised by high accessibility, high land values and limited space

**channel** the bed of a stream or river; also refers to the course or route that water flowing in a river takes

**climate** the average atmospheric weather conditions of a place over at least a thirty year period

**climate change** changes in the earth's weather, especially the increase in the temperature of the earth's atmosphere that is caused by the increase of particular gases, especially carbon dioxide

**coastal margin** the transition area between ocean and land, such as shallow coastal waters, beaches, dunelands, lowland rivers, estuaries, saltmarsh, and adjacent land areas

**colonisation** the system or policy by which one country maintains control or governance over a dependent nation, territory or people

**commercial** any activity or enterprise established with the intention of making a financial profit

**confluence** the meeting point of two or more streams or rivers

**continent** one of the seven main landmasses of the earth (Europe, Asia, Africa, North America, South America, Australia and Antarctica)

**continental shelf** the seabed bordering the continents, which is covered by shallow water – usually of less than 200 m. Along some coastlines the continental shelf is so narrow it is almost absent

**corrie** a bowl-shaped hollow found in upland glaciated areas

**crude oil** (or petroleum) is any naturally occurring flammable mixture of hydrocarbons found in geologic formations, such as rock strata

## D

**death rate** the number of people who die per 1000 of the population per year

**Demographic Transition Model** a graph that describes how populations change from high birth and death rates to low birth and death rates over time

**drainage ditch** a long, narrow trench or furrow dug into the ground to help remove water from the land

**drumlin** a low, oval hill formed from glacial deposits

## E

**earthquake** a movement or tremor of the earth's crust. The crust is subjected to tremendous stress. The rocks are forced to bend, and eventually the stress is so great that the rocks 'snap' along a faultline

**economic development** is the building up of prosperity and wealth of countries, regions or communities for the benefit of the people who live there

**economy** the production and consumption of goods and services and the supply of money within a country

**epicentre** the point on the earth's surface directly above the focus of an earthquake

**erratic** a boulder that is different to the surrounding rock and has been transported by glaciers

**Everest Base Camp** a term used to describe two base camps either side of Mount Everest. South Base Camp is in Nepal at an altitude of 5364 m and North Base Camp is in Tibet at an altitude of 5150 m

**Exclusive Economic Zone (EEZ)** an area of coastal water and seabed within a certain distance of a country's coastline, to which the country claims exclusive rights for fishing, drilling, and other economic activities

**exploitation** making use of and benefitting from resources

**exports** any goods or services sold to another country and shipped overseas

**extensive farming** is where a relatively small amount of produce is generated from a large area of farmland

## F

**fallow** farmland which is ploughed but left for a period without being sown in order to restore its fertility

**faultline** a fracture in the earth's crust on either side of which the rocks have been relatively displaced

**fertility rate** the average number of children born to a woman over her lifetime

**flood management** all methods used by people to try to reduce or prevent the negative effects of flood waters

**flood plain** an area of low-lying ground adjacent to a river, formed mainly of river sediments and subject to flooding

**fluvial** refers to the processes associated with rivers and streams and the deposits and landforms created by them

**focus** the location where an earthquake begins. The ground ruptures at this spot, then seismic waves radiate outwards in all directions

**fodder crops** crops that are cultivated primarily for animal feed

**freeze-thaw** a form of physical weathering where water enters cracks in the rock and then freezes during the night. This causes the crack to expand and then contract again during the day when the ice melts

## G

**Geographical Information Systems (GIS)** digital base maps with different layers of information added over the top. They are used by geographers to see display information and patterns, identify issues and make decisions. Google Earth is a basic example of a GIS

**geology** the study of the origin, history and structure of the earth

**glacial** a period of time where the extent of ice coverage is great. Also known as an Ice Age

**glacial trough** a U-shaped valley which has been eroded by glaciers in lowland areas

**glacier** a body of ice occupying a valley and originating in a corrie or icefield

**gorge** a narrow valley or pass between hills or mountains, typically with steep rocky walls and a stream running through it

**gross domestic product (GDP)** the total value of all goods and services produced domestically by a nation during a year

**Gulf Stream** a warm ocean current that begins in the Gulf of Mexico and flows northwards through the Atlantic Ocean

## H

**habitat** the natural home or environment of an animal, plant, or other organism

**hanging valley** a valley which is cut across by a deeper valley so that it looks to be hanging above the main valley floor

**harbour** a place on the coast where ships may moor in shelter, especially one protected from rough water by piers, jetties, and other artificial structures

**hard engineering schemes** involve high tech and often expensive human-made solutions to managing issues such as coastal erosion and river flooding

**hazard** a threat (natural or human) that has the potential to cause loss of life, injury, property damage, social impacts and damage to the environment

**headwater** the area where rain water collects and forms the small streams which eventually combine to create a large river as they flow down to lower land

**hemisphere** half of the earth, divided by the equator into the northern and southern hemispheres

**human geography** concerned with all the ways in which humans interact with their environment

## I

**Ice Age** an extremely cold period during which glaciers and ice sheets covered large areas of the planet

**imports** any goods or services purchased and brought into a country from abroad

**immigrant** a person who comes to live permanently in a foreign country

**incentive** a thing that motivates or encourages someone to do something

**indigenous people** people who have specific rights based on their historical and cultural ties to a particular place or territory

**Industrial Revolution** a period of industrialisation which happened in Britain in the eighteenth and nineteenth centuries and quickly spread to other parts of the world

**infant mortality** the number of babies under 1 year old that die per 1000 per year

**infrastructure** the basic make up of an area including, for example, roads, railways, schools, power and water supplies and drainage systems

**interglacial** a period of milder climate between two glacial periods. These are the climatic conditions that the earth is currently experiencing

## J

**jungle** an area of land overgrown with dense forest and tangled vegetation, typically in the tropics

## L

**lagoon** a stretch of salt water separated from the sea by a low sandbank or coral reef

**landslide** the mass movement of rock material, soil, etc. down the side of a mountain or cliff

**life expectancy** the average age that a person is expected to live

**liquefaction** a process where soil loses strength and acts like a fluid. Water is forced up through the soil through intense shaking during earthquakes. This intensifies seismic waves and increases damage of earthquakes

## M

**magma** hot fluid or semi-fluid material below or within the earth's crust from which lava and other igneous rock is formed on cooling

**marginal environment** land of poor quality because of lack of nutrients, soil erosion, distance from market or a lack of resources, which offers little or no potential for human activity

**median age** the average age of the population; half of the population is older, half of the population is younger

**migration** the movement of people or animals involving a permanent or semi-permanent change of residence

**moorland** open land usually with peaty soil covered with heather and bracken and moss

**moraine** rocks and sediment carried by glaciers and then deposited in lowland areas, usually at the sides or the end of the valley

**mouth** a part of a river where it flows into the sea, river, lake, reservoir or ocean

## N

**national park** an area of countryside, or occasionally sea or fresh water, protected by the state for the enjoyment of the general public and/or the conservation of the environment and wildlife

**natural change** a measure of how quickly

the population is growing or declining. Calculated by taking the death rate away from the birth rate

**natural gas** a flammable gas, consisting largely of methane and other hydrocarbons, occurring naturally underground (often in association with petroleum) and used as fuel

**natural resources** materials or substances occurring in nature which can be exploited for economic gain

**net migration** the difference between the number of people moving into a country (immigrants) and the number of people leaving a country (emigrants). If net migration is positive then there are more people coming into the country than leaving it whilst a negative figure suggests that there are more people leaving than coming in

## O

**open cast (strip) mining** the process of removing natural resources from the earth by excavating down from the surface of the land

**overfishing** to deplete the stock of fish in an area of sea by fishing excessively

## P

**Pacific Ring of Fire** an area where a large number of earthquakes and volcanic eruptions occur in the basin of the Pacific Ocean

**pasture** land covered with grass and other low plants suitable for grazing animals, especially cattle or sheep

**physical geography** concerned with natural features of the earth's surface such as landforms, rivers, climates, soils and vegetation

**plate boundary** where two tectonic plates meet. The Mid-Atlantic Ridge is where the Eurasian and North American plates meet. There are three main types:

conservative (transform) boundaries where plates move side by side relative to each other. Land is neither created or destroyed. Significant earthquakes can occur here, e.g. the Alpine Fault in New Zealand

constructive (divergent) boundaries where two plates are pulling apart and new crust is created. This leads to smaller earthquakes and volcanic activity, e.g. the Mid-Atlantic Ridge and the Rift Valley of East Africa

destructive (convergent) boundaries where plates move towards each other and one plate is subducted under another and melts. This leads to volcanoes, earthquakes and risks from tsunamis, e.g. the Pacific and Eurasian boundary off the east coast of Japan

**plate tectonics** the theory that the earth's crust is divided into seven large, rigid plates, and several smaller ones, which are moving relative to each other over the upper layers of the earth's mantle

**Pleistocene** the time period that began 1.8 million years ago and ended about 11,700 years ago

**plucking** this process of erosion occurs when glacial meltwater freezes onto the bedrock. As the glacier moves downslope it pulls, or plucks, chunks of rock with it

**population density** the average number of people living in each square kilometre of an area

**population distribution** the overall pattern of where people are living in an area

**pyramidal peak** a sharply pointed peak of a mountain which has been formed by three or more corries cutting back to back

## R

**Ramsar site** wetlands of international importance, recognised globally due to the Ramsar Convention, which is an international treaty for the conservation and wise use of wetlands

**region** an area (e.g. a part of a country or the world) having definable characteristics but not always fixed boundaries

**relief** the general height and shape of the landscape in an area

**replacement rate** a total fertility rate of 2.1 means that the population will be stable (assuming there is no migration)

# Glossary

**residential red zone** an area of housing in Christchurch, NZ heavily damaged by the 2011 earthquake liquefaction. It cannot be used for housing in the future and all residents have been forced to leave

**resilience** the capacity to cope with or recover quickly from difficulties or challenges

**ribbon lake** a long, narrow lake formed by glacial erosion

**Richter Scale** a logarithmic scale used to measure the magnitude of earthquakes. A magnitude 7 earthquake is ten times more powerful than a magnitude 6 and 100 times more powerful than a magnitude 5

## S

**seismologist** a person who studies earthquakes

**semi-arid** refers to places with low and often irregular annual rainfall of between 250–500 mm that are often susceptible to droughts

**settlement** any place of any size where people decide to live such as a farmstead or huge city

**shield volcano** a broad-domed volcano composed of non-viscous lava which flows quickly and congeals slowly, producing gently sloping slides

**Site of Special Scientific Interest (SSSI)** an environmentally important and protected area of conservation in the United Kingdom

**soft engineering schemes** involve low-tech and often cheaper and more sustainable solutions to environmental management issues through working with natural processes

**spatial concentration** observations made to describe the geographic patterns of features, both physical and human across the earth

**Special Protection Area (SPA)** an area designated under the European Union Directive on the Conservation of Wild Birds. All member states have a duty to safeguard these habitats of migratory birds and certain particularly threatened birds

**spur** a ridge of land descending from a hill towards lower land or a valley

**subduction zone** where one more dense oceanic tectonic plate plunges beneath a continental plate at a destructive plate boundary.

**Sub-Saharan Africa** the part of the continent of Africa which lies south of the Sahara Desert

**sustainability** development that meets the needs of the present without impacting negatively on the environment or compromising the ability of future generations to meet their own needs

**sustainable** able to be maintained at a certain rate or level

## T

**tarn** a small, circular lake found in the bottom of corries

**tourism** the commercial organisation and operation of holidays and visits to places of interest

**trade** the action of buying and selling goods and services between countries around the world

**transport** the means by which people and goods are moved from one place to another by means of a road vehicle, train, aircraft or ship

**treaty** a formal agreement between states that has been concluded and ratified

**tributary** a river or stream flowing into a larger river or lake

**tsunami** a very large, and often destructive, sea wave produced by a submarine earthquake

## U

**United Nations Convention on the Law of the Sea (UNCLOS)** signed in 1982, this has so far been the best attempt to agree how nations should govern the world's oceans

**urban** a built up area such as a town or city

## V

**valley** a low area of land between hills or mountains, typically with a river or stream flowing through it

## Y

**youthful population** a population which has a large number of people under the age of 1

# Index

Note: page numbers in bold refer to maps.

# Index

# Index

# Acknowledgements

The publishers wish to thank the following for permission to reproduce photographs, illustrations and other graphics. Every effort has been made to trace copyright holders and to obtain their permission for the use of copyright materials. The publishers will gladly receive any information enabling them to rectify any error or omission at the first opportunity.

Contains Ordnance Survey data © Crown copyright and database right 2014
© Crown copyright and database rights (2014) Ordnance Survey (100018598)

We acknowledge the New Zealand GeoNet project and its sponsors EQC, GNS Science and LINZ, for providing data/images used in this study.

Contains public sector information licensed under the Open Government Licence v1.0

Illustrations by Jouve Pvt Ltd pp 13, 15, 24, 54

Images: (t = top, c= center, b= bottom, r – right, l = left)
Cover and tile page image © Arina P Habich/Shutterstock.com; p4 (tl) © INTERFOTO/Alamy; p4 (cl) © www.BibleLandPictures.com/Alamy; p5 (cr) © Richard Levine/Alamy; p5 (bl) © Festa/Shutterstock.com; p5 (b) © Xinhua/Alamy; p6 (t) © North Wind Picture Archives/Alamy; p6 (b) © Art Directors & TRIP/Alamy; p8 (tl) © ixpert/Shutterstock.com; p8 (cl) © NOWAK LUKASZ/Shutterstock.com; p8 (b) Data from © U.S. Department of the Interior/USGS; p9 (t) © IndianSummer/Shutterstock.com; p10 (c) © Smith609/Wikimedia Commons CC BY 3.0; p11 (t) © Katarina Christenson/Shutterstock.com; p11 (b) © albinoni/Shutterstock.com; p12 (b) © Moviestore collection Ltd/Alamy; p13 (t) © Walter Siegmund/Wikimedia Commons CC BY 2.5; p14 (l) © Fedor Selivanov/Shutterstock.com; p14 (b) © Brendan Howard/Shutterstock.com; p15 (cr) © Stewart Smith Photography/Shutterstock.com; p17 (b) © Ordnance Survey 2014 (100018598); p18 (bl) © Gilles Baechler/Shutterstock.com; p19 (cl) © Matt Gibson/Shutterstock.com; p19 (cr) © romanophoto.com/Shutterstock.com; p19 (bl) © Eric Jones/Geograph.org.uk CC BY-SA 2.0; p19 (br) © dubassy/Shutterstock.com; p20 (cl) © Seb Hutchings; p20 (bl) © Gareth Williams; p20 (b) © Drew Rawcliffe/Shutterstock.com; p21 © Peter Burgess; p22 (cr) © Avatar_023/Shutterstock.com; p22 (b) © Burben / Shutterstock.com; p23 (t) © bikeriderlondon/Shutterstock.com; p23 (c) © Gary Whitton/Shutterstock.com; p25 (t) © ITAR-TASS Photo Agency/Alamy; p26 (tl) © Oleksiy Avtomonov/Shutterstock.com; p26 (b) © Steve Allen/Shutterstock.com; p27 (t) © Jan Miko / Shutterstock.com; p27 (b) © Leonid Ikan/Shutterstock.com; p28 (bl) © fotomak/Shutterstock.com; p27 (bc) © Svetlana Arapova/Shutterstock.com; p28 (br) © Radiokafka/Shutterstock.com; p29 (t) © ChameleonsEye/Shutterstock.com; p29 (cr) © Vlad Karavaev/Shutterstock.com; p29 (br) © Sylvie Bouchard/Shutterstock.com; p31 (c) © Alfred Renow/Martin Edström Studios; p31 (tr) © Daniel Prudek/Shutterstock.com; p31 (cr) © Daniel Prudek/Shutterstock.com; p32, p33 © Sustainable Tourism Development Project, Ministry of Information, Culture and Tourism of Lao PDR 2014; p34 (c) © Awing88/Wikimedia Commons CC BY-SA 3.0; p34 (b) © Chief Yeoman Alphonso Braggs, US-Navy/Wikimedia Commons; p35 (t) © Jesse Allen/NASA Earth Observatory; p35 (b) © NOAA/climate.gov; p36 (tl) © Mike Campbell/flickr.com CC BY-ND 2.0; p36 (cl) © Greg O'Beirne/flickr.com; p36 (t) © Nicholas Sheehan; p37 (b) © Chris Mance/GeoNet; p39 (c) © NASA's Visible Earth; p39 (x11) © Nicholas Sheehan; p40 (tr) © Mikenorton/Wikimedia Commons CC BY-SA 3.0; p41 (c) © GeoNet; p41 (b) © GeoNet; p42 (t), p42 (cl) © Nicholas Sheehan; p42 (b) © NigelSpiers/Shutterstock.com; p44 (t) © GeoNet; p44 (tl), p44 (cl) © Schwede66/Wikimedia Commons CC BY 3.0; p44 (bl) © Greg O'Beirne/Wikimedia Commons CC BY-SA 3.0; p47 (tl), p47 (tr), p47 (cr) © Nicholas Sheehan; p47 (cl) © Gabriel Goh/flickr.com CC BY 2.0; p47 (bl) © New Zealand Defence Force; p47 (br) © NigelSpiers/Shutterstock.com; p48 (t), p48 (cl), p48 (bl), p49 (cl), p49 (cr) © Nicholas Sheehan; p50 (c) © Canterbury Earthquake Recovery Authority (CERA); p52 (tl) © Expedition 34 crew/NASA Earth Observatory; p52 (bl) © Expedition 19 crew/NASA Earth Observatory; p52 (c) © Jeff Schmaltz MODIS Land Rapid Response Team/NASA GSFC; p53 (tr) © Jeff Schmaltz MODIS Land Rapid Response Team/NASA GSFC; p53 (tcr) © NASA World Wind; p53 (bcr) © Jacques Descloitres MODIS Land Rapid Response Team/NASA GSFC; p53 (br) © Jeff Schmaltz MODIS Land Rapid Response Team/NASA GSFC; p53 (c) © MODIS Rapid Response System/NASA; p54 (c) © NASA Landsat; p54 (b) © Johnson Space Center/NASA Earth Observatory; p56 (tl) © Cambridge Aerial Photography/Alamy; p56 (cl) © Jack Sullivan/Alamy; p56 (bl) © LatitudeStock/Alamy; p57 (t) © Living with a Changing Coast (LiCCo); p57 (b) © Crown copyright and database right 2014; p58 (t) © Living with a Changing Coast (LiCCo); p58 (b) © John Farmar/Alamy; p59 © 2014 Ordnance Survey (100018598); p60 (tl) © David Weatherly; p60 (tcl) © Angie Sharp/Alamy; p60 (bcl) © Jinny Goodman /Alamy; p60 (bl) © Carolyn Jenkins/Alamy; p61 (t) © l iving with a Changing Coast (LiCCo); p61 (tr) © dbphots/Alamy; p61 (cr) © Dom Greves/Alamy; p61 (br) © Bob Gibbons/Alamy; p62 (cl) © FLPA/Alamy; p62 (c) © Arterra Picture Library/Alamy; p62 (cr) © Andrew Darrington /Alamy; p62 (bl) © Avico Ltd/Alamy; p62 (b) © avid tipling/Alamy; p62 (br) © mike lane/Alamy; p63 (x6) © David Weatherly; p64 (t) © David Weatherly; p64 (bl) © David Weatherly; p65 (t) © dbphots/Alamy; p65 (cr) © David Weatherly; p65 (b) © Dom Greves/Alamy; p65 (br) © David Weatherly; p66 (t) Data from © U.S. EPA Climate Change Website; p66 (b) © Giorgiogp2/NOAA Laboratory for Satellite Atimertry; p67 (tr) © Oikos-team/Wikimedia Commons; p67 (tcr) © Mark Gadsby/Geograph.org.uk; p67 (cr) © Mike Goldwater/Alamy; p67 (bcr) © Pix/Alamy; p67 (cr) © Alex Segre/Alamy; p67 (c) © J.R. Bale/Alamy; p67 (b) © FLPA/Alamy; p69 (tr) © Simon Colmer/Alamy; p70 (c) © Universal Images Group Limited/Alamy; p71 Data from Australian Bureau of Statistics; p73 © 1995, WORLDSAT International and J. Knighton/Science Photo Library; p74 (tl) © Materialscientist/Wikimedia Commons; p74 (tc) © State Library of New South Wales/Wikimedia Commons; p74 (bc) © John Oxley Library, State Library of Queensland; p74 (bl) © National Library of Australia Collection/Wikimedia Commons; p74 (br) © A Narrative of the Expedition to Botany Bay, Watkin Tench 1789; p75 (tr) © Thomas Larcom/Wikimedia Commons; p76 (tl) © Reto Stöckl/NASA Goddard Space Flight Center; p77 (c) © Peripitus/Wikimedia Commons CC BY-SA 3.0; p77 (b) © Bidgee/Wikimedia Commons CC BY-SA 3.0; p78 (t) © The Print Collector/Alamy; p78 (tr) © Richard Daintree/Wikimedia Commons; p78 (c) © Edward Roper/Wikimedia Commons; p79 (tr) © Rob Lavinsky/Wikimedia Commons CC BY-SA 3.0; p79 (bl) © Graham Corney/Alamy; p79 (br) © Brian Voon Yee Yap/Wikimedia Commons CC BY-SA 3.0; p80 © National Archives of Australia/Wikimedia Commons; p81 © Commonwealth of Australia/Wikimedia Commons; p82 (tl) © MagSpace/Shutterstock.com; p82 (tcl) © Phillip Minnis/Shutterstock.com; p82 (bcl) © Robyn Mackenzie/Shutterstock.com; 82 (bl) © Manfred Gottschalk/Alamy; p83 (tr) © Vinayaraj/Wikimedia Commons CC BY-SA 3.0; p84 (t) © Five Years/Wikimedia Commons CC BY-SA 3.0; p84 (tl) © Bäras/Wikimedia Commons CC BY-SA 3.0; p84 (bl) © Edward Haylan/Shutterstock.com; p84 (b) © Adwo/Shutterstock.com; p85 (tr) © Rolf Richardson/Alamy; p85 (tcr) © Geez-oz/Wikimedia Commons CC BY-SA 3.0; p85 (cr) © Photoshot Holdings Ltd/Alamy; p85 (bcr) © Calistemon/Wikimedia Commons CC BY-SA 3.0; p85 (br) © Calistemon/Wikimedia Commons CC BY-SA 3.0; p85 (b) © Tor Lindstrand/Australian Vernacular/flickr.com CC BY-SA 2.0; p86 (b) © Australian Bureau of Statistics, 2006 & 2011 Censuses of Population and Housing; p88 (tl) © ian woolcock/Alamy; p89 (t) © paul weston/Alamy; p89 (cl) © Christopher Nicholson/Alamy; p89 (cr) © Google Earth; p89 (bl) © DavidYoung/Shutterstock.com; p89 (br) © Christopher Nicholson/Alamy; p90 © Ordnance Survey 2014 (100018598); p91 (c), p91 (b), p92 (tl), p92 (tr), p92 (cl), p92 (cr), p92 (bl), p92 (br) © David Weatherly; p93 (cl) © FLPA/Alamy; p93 (r) © FLPA/Alamy; p93 (b) © Martin Fowler/Alamy; p94 (tl) © MetOffice; p94 (b) © photosilta/Alamy; p95 (cl) © Daily Mail/Rex/Alamy; p95 (cr) © Adam Burton/Alamy; p95 (bl) © The National Trust Photolibrary/Alamy; p95 (br) © Trinity Mirror/Mirrorpix /Alamy; p96 (tl) © Daily Mail/Rex/Alamy; p96 (tr) © Daily Mail/Rex/Alamy; p96 (c) © Daily Mail/Rex/Alamy; p96 (bl) © Trinity Mirror/Mirrorpix/Alamy; p96 (br) © Daily Mail/Rex/Alamy; p98 (tl) © Prisma Bildagentur AG/Alamy; p98 (tr) © Daily Mail/Rex/Alamy; p98 (cl) © Chronicle/Alamy; p98 (cr) © Science Photo Library/Alamy; p98 (bl) © Mike Charles/Shutterstock.com; p98 (br) © Daily Mail/Rex/Alamy; p99 Ordnance Survey 2014 (100018598); p100 (t) © dbphots/Alamy; p100 (c) © Ruth Sharville/Geograph.org.uk CC BY-SA 2.0; p100 (cr) © Sebastian Wasek/Alamy; p100 (bl) © Google Earth; p100 (br) © geogphotos/Alamy; p101 (tr) © David Weatherly; p102 (tl), p102 (tcl), p102 (bcl), p102 (bl) © National Trust; p103 (t), p103 (b) © National Trust; p104 (t), p104 (c), p104 (b) © National Trust; p105 (tr) © National Trust; p106 (tl) © D. Sharon Pruitt/Wikimedia Commons; p108 (tl) © Wlad74/Shutterstock.com; p108 (cl) © Shootov/Shutterstock.com; p110 (bl) © Warren Goldswain/Shutterstock.com; p110 (br) © v. schlichting/Shutterstock.com; p111 (tl) © Christian Delbert/Shutterstock.com; p111 (c) © Sundraw Photography/Shutterstock.com; p111 (tr) © Pressmaster/Shutterstock.com; p111 (cr) © Tom Gowanlock/Shutterstock.com; p111 (br) © Andrey_Popov/Shutterstock.com; p112 (b) © Mila Supinskaya/Shutterstock.com, p113 (cl) © Richard Peterson/Shutterstock.com; p113 (cr) © Africa Studio/Shutterstock.com; p115 (tr © Goran Bogicevic/Shutterstock.com; p115 (cr) © Monkey Business Images/Shutterstock.com; p116 (b) © koya979/Shutterstock.com; p117 (b) © bikeriderlondon/Shutterstock.com